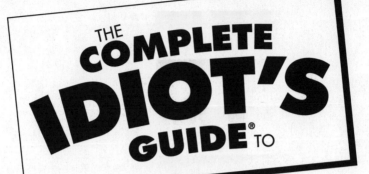

THE

COMPLETE
IDIOT'S
GUIDE® TO

Soccer
Basics

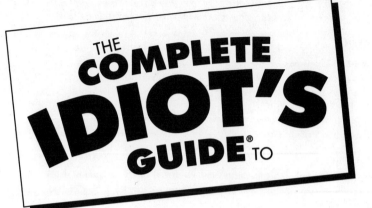

Soccer
Basics

by Sam Borden

ALPHA

A member of Penguin Group (USA) Inc.

To my father, John, who watched me play so many games in so many places; and to my mother, Marian, who made me want to write about them.

ALPHA BOOKS

Published by the Penguin Group

Penguin Group (USA) Inc., 375 Hudson Street, New York, New York 10014, USA

Penguin Group (Canada), 90 Eglinton Avenue East, Suite 700, Toronto, Ontario M4P 2Y3, Canada (a division of Pearson Penguin Canada Inc.)

Penguin Books Ltd., 80 Strand, London WC2R 0RL, England

Penguin Ireland, 25 St. Stephen's Green, Dublin 2, Ireland (a division of Penguin Books Ltd.)

Penguin Group (Australia), 250 Camberwell Road, Camberwell, Victoria 3124, Australia (a division of Pearson Australia Group Pty. Ltd.)

Penguin Books India Pvt. Ltd., 11 Community Centre, Panchsheel Park, New Delhi—110 017, India

Penguin Group (NZ), 67 Apollo Drive, Rosedale, North Shore, Auckland 1311, New Zealand (a division of Pearson New Zealand Ltd.)

Penguin Books (South Africa) (Pty.) Ltd., 24 Sturdee Avenue, Rosebank, Johannesburg 2196, South Africa

Penguin Books Ltd., Registered Offices: 80 Strand, London WC2R 0RL, England

Copyright © 2009 by Sam Borden

THE COMPLETE IDIOT'S GUIDE TO and Design are registered trademarks of Penguin Group (USA) Inc.

International Standard Book Number: 978-1-59257-830-6
Library of Congress Catalog Card Number: 2008933147

11   10   8   7   6   5   4   3   2

Interpretation of the printing code: The rightmost number of the first series of numbers is the year of the book's printing; the rightmost number of the second series of numbers is the number of the book's printing. For example, a printing code of 09-1 shows that the first printing occurred in 2009.

Printed in the United States of America

Note: This publication contains the opinions and ideas of its author. It is intended to provide helpful and informative material on the subject matter covered. It is sold with the understanding that the author and publisher are not engaged in rendering professional services in the book. If the reader requires personal assistance or advice, a competent professional should be consulted.

The author and publisher specifically disclaim any responsibility for any liability, loss, or risk, personal or otherwise, which is incurred as a consequence, directly or indirectly, of the use and application of any of the contents of this book.

Most Alpha books are available at special quantity discounts for bulk purchases for sales promotions, premiums, fundraising, or educational use. Special books, or book excerpts, can also be created to fit specific needs.

For details, write: Special Markets, Alpha Books, 375 Hudson Street, New York, NY 10014.

Publisher: *Marie Butler-Knight*
Editorial Director/Acquiring Editor: *Mike Sanders*
Senior Managing Editor: *Billy Fields*
Development Editor: *Megan Douglass*
Production Editor: *Kayla Dugger*
Copy Editor: *Tricia Liebig*

Cartoonist: *Steve Barr*
Cover Designer: *Rebecca Harmon*
Book Designer: *Trina Wurst*
Indexer: *Celia McCoy*
Layout: *Chad Dressler*
Proofreader: *Mary Hunt*

Contents at a Glance

Contents

Introduction

Soccer memories linger. I mean, I still remember everything about my first soccer team. We were called the Aztecs and we played in my town's recreational league. We had blue and yellow reversible jerseys and blue shorts. I was in third grade.

Saturdays were fantastic back then. It was game day, which meant putting on my uniform, running around until I got a cramp in my side, and then sucking on an orange slice at halftime. Sometimes we got donut holes to eat after the game. It was heaven.

Kids all over the country are having experiences like mine every weekend. Soccer is the most popular sport in the world and it's steadily growing in America, too, especially as hordes of children are becoming attached to the game at a young age. As they grow, so, too, will soccer.

Truth is, it's hard to shake soccer when you get hooked. At some point in the middle of that season with the Aztecs, I took a turn playing goalie and loved it. I asked my parents to get me a pair of goalie gloves and, for the better part of the next 15 years, I devoted myself to making as many saves as I could.

I tried out for a travel team, some select teams, and was picked to join an elite team of players from around the country that traveled to England and Sweden one summer. I was co-captain of my high school varsity team and became a coach and certified referee. In college I played for my fraternity team and then joined several adult leagues after I graduated. I just enjoyed being around the game.

Soccer has always struck me as being fluid and rhythmic. There are no long pauses between pitches, no long breaks for free throws, and no huddling up after every play. The game moves and breathes and flows. It's dramatic and exciting and relaxing all at the same time.

I remember moments from nearly all the seasons I played—some good, some bad—and I can still run my own personal highlight reel in my head at any moment. Once, when I was about 7 years old, I made a diving save on a free kick that one of my best friends took; we still joke about it today, more than two decades later.

Maybe you're reading this book because your child wants to start playing. Or because you want to start playing. Or because you saw a soccer game on TV and want to know more.

The reality is that the reason doesn't matter much. All that matters is that you're doing it. Congratulations! It won't be long before you have soccer memories, too.

Inside This Book

This book is broken into four parts, so feel free to jump in at the part that seems most appropriate to you.

If you're looking for an overview of the game so you can be a semi-knowledgeable soccer mom or dad, **Part 1, "Pregame Prep,"** will give you a general breakdown of how the game works and how to find a place for your child to play.

In **Part 2, "Crime and Punishment: The Laws of the Game,"** we cover the rules: what's allowed and what isn't, plus all the different types of free kicks and other violations that might take place during the game. There's also a section on referees that'll help you understand how a game is officiated, as well as some candid advice on what parents and coaches can say to refs if they have questions about the calls.

Part 3, "Practice Makes Perfect," is the meat of the book because it's full of information (and pictures!) related to the basic soccer skills. Everything is covered here: dribbling, passing, trapping, shooting, and (of course) playing goalie, complete with fun games and drills that will help practice what's been learned.

Part 4, "Saturday in the Park," is a game day primer for parents. How early to leave for the field, what kind of stretching players should do to avoid getting hurt, how to be a linesman, and the best kind of halftime snacks are just a few of the topics covered. You'll also get some tips on how to deal with your child's coach and how to tell if your kid is having a good game.

Extras

As you make your way through this book, you'll find a few different boxes full of info:

def•i•ni•tion

These are words that are part of the soccer language. Use these boxes and the glossary at the end of the book to stay on top of the lingo.

Yellow Card

Every sport has its pitfalls. These boxes serve as warnings of things that might trip you up before, during, or after the game.

Throw-Ins

A story, a factoid, or just something I thought you'd want to know. These are little bits of soccer candy that you don't need but might find interesting anyway.

WELL DONE!

Instead of saying "good job," one of my first coaches always said "well done!" As I quickly learned, lots of coaches use this phrase (especially British ones), so these boxes have coaching tips just for parents.

Acknowledgments

Writing a book about soccer is, apparently, much more difficult than actually playing soccer, so I would like to take a moment to give thanks …

To my best friend from college (and favorite roommate), Michael Osborne, who brainstormed the initial table of contents for this book with me; to my agent, Bob Diforio, for suggesting me for the project; to Mike Sanders, Megan Douglass, Kayla Dugger, Tricia Liebig, and the Alpha Books group for their wisdom and support; to my brothers, Charles and Dan, and my sister, Maggie, for being such superstars; to my brother-in-law, Brad, and my sister-in-law, Rebecca, for clearly being worthy of joining the team; to my in-laws, Pam and Rick, for giving me love and support and the most beautiful woman in the world; and to Jessica, for being all I could ever want.

Trademarks

All terms mentioned in this book that are known to be or are suspected of being trademarks or service marks have been appropriately capitalized. Alpha Books and Penguin Group (USA) Inc. cannot attest to the accuracy of this information. Use of a term in this book should not be regarded as affecting the validity of any trademark or service mark.

Part 1

Pregame Prep

So you've heard of soccer before but don't know much about it. Or you've seen it on TV a few times and have a basic understanding, but don't really know much about how to play. Or maybe you're still trying to figure out where the yard-lines and first-down markers are.

Chapter 1 covers the basics, from how the game is played to what kind of shopping list you'll need for your soccer-playing son or daughter. Chapter 2 helps you pick out a league and team for your child—including a section on how to handle tryouts for a travel team—and Chapter 3 gives you information on outfitting your new athlete with everything from shirts to cleats. Chapter 4 then gives you an overview of the field and game setup, so you'll know what you're watching when you show up on Saturday morning.

1

Soccer 101

In This Chapter

- ◆ The bare essentials of the game
- ◆ Soccer's beginnings
- ◆ The growth of the sport in America
- ◆ The cost of doing business as a soccer parent

Soccer is the world's most popular sport, though most Americans probably don't know it. Football, baseball, and basketball dominate the scene here, but even though soccer hasn't caught up to those three on the professional level in the United States, there's no denying the popularity of soccer among children. Everywhere you look, kids are playing.

Will those massive numbers of young players continue to follow soccer as they get older, eventually making it a premier sport in America? No one knows for sure, but it's obvious that understanding soccer is quickly becoming a requirement for parents of kids who want to join the fun.

Kids can start playing forms of soccer as soon as they're able to run, and most towns have teams for almost any age—from preschool on up to adult leagues. Some are recreational and others are more competitive; all should end up being a lot of fun.

The Object of the Game

The point of a soccer game is for your team to score more goals than the opponent. A goal is scored when the ball passes between the two goal posts and underneath the crossbar. Each goal counts as one, regardless of where the shooter is on the field. There is no such thing as a three-pointer.

Typically, soccer is not a particularly high-scoring sport. This is one reason some experts believe it hasn't become as popular in America, but the truth is that those who understand soccer quickly realize that goals are far from the only exciting part of the game.

What Is Soccer?

If you're new to soccer, particularly if you're a parent who wants to figure out what you're seeing your kid do out there on the field with everyone else, there are seven basic concepts to remember. I call them the "Sacred Seven," and understanding them will give you a pretty good idea of what you're watching.

No. 1: Heaven Eleven

A soccer team has 11 players on the field. One of them is the *goalkeeper* or goalie, who stays close to the goal and tries to prevent the opposing team from scoring. The other 10 are field players who run more freely. The three basic types of positions are *fullbacks* (who primarily play defense), *forwards* (who primarily attack), and *midfielders* (who do both). We'll get into more specifics about each type of position in Chapter 4, but that's the basic breakdown of a soccer team.

Each team also has a varying number of substitutes (usually no more than six or seven). In professional games, substitutes are rare because a player who is replaced can't re-enter the game. But in most youth leagues teams are allowed to substitute freely and players can go in and out of the game as often as the coach wants.

def•i•ni•tion

The **goalkeeper** is the only player who can use his hands, and is primarily responsible for keeping the opposing team from scoring. **Fullbacks** are a team's main defenders, and spend much of the game in their own half protecting their goal. **Forwards** (sometimes called *strikers*) are a team's main attackers and spend much of the game in the opponent's half of the field. **Midfielders** (sometimes called *halfbacks*) play in between and help on both offense and defense.

No. 2: Keep Your Hands Clean

Soccer players don't use their hands or arms to touch the ball (unless they're the goalkeeper). They can use their feet, their thighs, their chest, and their head—all skills we'll get to in Part 3—but touching the ball with a hand or arm is against the rules (pretty much anything below the shoulder is considered the "hand"). If a player touches the ball with his hand, the referee will give a free kick to the other team.

No. 3: No Fighting, No Biting

Most of the things you think are illegal in soccer actually are. Players can't push, trip, grab, or hold other players, and they're certainly not allowed to punch, hit, or kick other players. That doesn't mean soccer isn't a physical game though; bumping another player's shoulder with your own shoulder as you battle for the ball is allowed, and there is always plenty of jostling for position all over the field.

No. 4: Inside Offside

The most complicated rule in soccer is offside, and that's why there's a whole chapter dedicated to it in Part 2. Here's the simplest way to say it: if a player has less than two opponents—*including the goalie*—between him and the goal he's attacking at the time a teammate passes him the ball, he's offside. Is it an odd rule? Yes. Does it serve a purpose? Yes. This is about as basic an explanation as you can get, and it's plenty for most casual spectators. If you want to understand more about offside, turn to Chapter 7.

The basic premise behind the offside rule is to keep forwards from just hanging out near the opponent's goal and waiting for someone to pass them the ball. By saying that there must be two opponents—typically one defender and the goalie—between the attacker and the goal, teams are forced to use more precise passes and dribbling to try and score.

No. 5: Running on Empty

There is a lot of running in soccer. A lot. More than you can probably imagine. During a typical professional match (which is 90 minutes long), players run an average of 7 miles. Obviously youth matches are shorter, but you get the point: make sure kids have stretched properly and drink *a lot* of water during the game. Afterward, they should drink even more and it's probably a good idea to spend some time off their feet to rest.

For more information on the length of matches, see Chapter 4.

No. 6: Size Doesn't Matter

Anyone can play soccer. There are no "he's not big enough to be a linebacker" requirements in this game, and as long you like running around, you can find a way to help a soccer team win. If you're shorter than average, maybe you'll end up being one of the quickest players on the field; if you're taller or broader, maybe you'll be the strongest defender or best header. Whatever your body type, soccer is a game for everyone.

No. 7: Fundamentals

Knowing how to do the basic moves in soccer—dribbling, passing, trapping, and shooting—are important because they're the backbone of the game. There are plenty of fun ways to practice these techniques, and getting better at them will make the games themselves that much more enjoyable. Even the most advanced soccer players spend most of their time working on the basics. Check out Part 3 for a skill-by-skill breakdown.

Everyone Else Calls It Football

It's not hard to understand why in England, France, and just about everywhere else in the world, soccer is called "football," right? This game has been around forever, and some historians believe the game's beginnings go as far back as the cavemen.

The Chinese had a soccerlike game called *tsu chu* which they played during an Emperor's birthday celebration around 2500 B.C.E., and soccer was played in a variety of forms—and with a variety of "balls," which included pig bladders, coconuts and other fruit, and even skulls—throughout history.

A more recognizable version of the game was developed in the 1800s, when an organization known as FIFA was formed to standardize the rules.

From Pele to Posh Spice

The current big-time professional soccer league in the United States is called Major League Soccer (or MLS), which has 14 teams in cities such as Los Angeles, Chicago, and New York. MLS isn't the first serious professional league in America though; that honor belongs to the now-defunct North American Soccer League (or NASL), which had its (limited) heyday in the 1970s and early 1980s. The New York Cosmos played a big part in that surge of success because they spent $4.5 million (remember this was more than 30 years ago!) on Pele, the Brazilian soccer star who was known worldwide.

The NASL folded in 1984 after overexpansion and an influx of too many international players saw its popularity plummet, leaving no top-level soccer league in the United States until 1996, when MLS was formed. Creating the new league was part of an agreement the United States Soccer Federation made with FIFA that allowed the United States to host the 1994 World Cup, a competition among the world's best national teams that is played every four years.

MLS has thrived in recent years, and in 2007 it welcomed a big international star of its own when David Beckham, whose celebrity was only matched by that of his wife, former Spice Girl Victoria, left England to join the Los Angeles Galaxy. His arrival is just one indication that the rest of the world is taking professional soccer in the United States very seriously once again.

Money Talks

I played hockey as a kid, in addition to soccer, and with the skates, shoulder pads, leg pads, helmet, and everything else, it's no contest which sport cost my parents more money. In fact, compared to just about every other sport, soccer is an incredible bargain.

Prices for equipment can change so much from year to year (and store to store), but it's not unreasonable to believe you can outfit an average 10-year-old soccer player with everything she'll need for less than $100. You should also factor in the registration fee for whatever league your child might be playing in, or a membership fee if a local organization such as the YMCA is running the league. These fees can vary greatly from town to town, and may be required twice a year (in the fall and spring, if there are two seasons).

WELL DONE!

A well-planned carpool can be the difference between a maddeningly hectic weekend and one that everyone— kids and parents—actually enjoys. If you're juggling several different schedules for practices and games (plus your own life's demands), see if a carpool with one (or more) of your child's teammates might make everyone a little saner, as well as saving each family some money on gas.

The biggest expense for soccer moms and dads? It may well be gas. With the popularity of soccer booming, leagues and tournaments are being played all over the place, so there's a good chance you'll end up putting some decent miles on the car if your child ends up playing on a travel team. Trust me, it's still better than buying new skates every year.

A Basic Shopping List

Chapter 3 is all about how to choose the right equipment for your child—including cleats and shinguards—but there are also a variety of other items that could be part of your soccer spree.

Here's a basic shopping list to keep in mind when you're perusing the aisles at your local sporting goods emporium or soccer store:

◆ Cleats

◆ Shinguards

◆ Soccer ball

◆ Two pairs soccer shorts

◆ Two pairs soccer socks

◆ Athletic tape

◆ Sweatband/headband (to keep long hair out of the eyes)

◆ Water bottle

If you've got these items, you can play soccer. As players develop and get more serious, there may be other additions and accessories that become more attractive or necessary (ankle supports, for example, or a second set of cleats), but starting with this list ought to be plenty.

No Boys Allowed

Recent statistics show that more than 7 million women play soccer, most of them age 17 and younger. In many ways, women's soccer is as popular—if not more so—than men's soccer in America, particularly because of the success of the U.S. Women's National team.

When the U.S. team beat China to win the Women's World Cup in 1999, it was an incredibly dramatic moment (and one that will surely be remembered for U.S. player Brandi Chastain's celebration in her sports bra after ripping off her shirt in excitement).

WELL DONE!

What got lost in the hype over Brandi Chastain's reaction to winning the 1999 World Cup was the incredible game the Americans played to claim the trophy. Their effort in the whole tournament had been amazing, and Chastain's celebration reflected that. What did she say about tearing off her shirt? "Momentary insanity, nothing more, nothing less. I wasn't thinking about anything. I thought, 'This is the greatest moment of my life on the soccer field.'"

Even without the success of the women's national team, girls have been drawn to soccer. The majority of leagues and tournaments run all-girls divisions or brackets, and the competitiveness levels are typically identical to that of the boys.

Soccer is a universal game and the skills, tactics, and rules are essentially identical regardless of gender. Don't kid yourself: soccer is one of those games where a great girls' team would absolutely beat a bad boys' team in a game. Soccer is an equalizer—just another reason why it's the best sport around.

For more in-depth information on the game, see Chapter 4.

The Least You Need to Know

◆ Soccer is the world's most popular sport and it's growing all the time in America.

◆ Major League Soccer is the current professional league in America, and its recent success has increased its credibility around the globe.

◆ Outfitting your child with the proper equipment won't require you taking out a loan. Soccer's a relative sports bargain.

◆ Girls' soccer is just as popular as boys' soccer and, in many cases, the quality of play is even better.

Chapter 2

Where Should My Kid Play?

In This Chapter

- ◆ Introducing your child to soccer
- ◆ Picking a league
- ◆ Dealing with tryouts for travel and premier teams
- ◆ Considering the future

In most towns, finding a place for kids to play soccer is about as difficult as finding a Starbucks. Leagues abound, and most feature a wide variety of competition levels to make sure your child isn't over- or undermatched.

Possibilities can range from basic instruction classes to recreational leagues, from travel and select teams to Development Academy teams. The best way to find out what's right for your child is to start at the beginning.

Local Clinics

Some kids start playing soccer as young as age 4. For children just starting out with soccer, the best introduction is a clinic. Your local JCC or YMCA probably offers some sort of soccer class for a range of ages, with the focus on having fun while at the same time getting used to the idea of kicking the ball.

These classes, which are often run once or twice a week, mostly just give kids a chance to run around within the basic mold of a soccer game. Usually the organization running the program will use college students, recent graduates, or other skilled adults to lead the class, which typically features lots of games that focus on a particular skill.

The games are familiar—Red Rover, Red Light/Green Light, even Duck-Duck-Goose—but have a soccer ball inserted into the action. This gives kids lots of touches on the soccer ball and makes them more comfortable with the idea of dribbling, passing, or shooting.

The best way to find out about these kinds of clinics or classes is to call your local recreation department, JCC, or YMCA. Also ask around at the park or PTA meeting; word of mouth is a great way to find out information about the pluses and minuses of your town's offerings.

The Rec League

After your child has moved past the instruction stage, the next step is getting into a recreational league. The majority of towns run these leagues, which are broken down into divisions based on age (denoted as "Under 10" or "U10," for example, which means only players age 9 and younger can play in that league). The players are then put on teams and play a schedule of games against the other teams at local fields, typically on weekends.

The rec league is a great way to introduce your child to competition in soccer, because most rec leagues

> **WELL DONE!**
>
> It's common to see boys and girls playing together at younger ages and in noncompetitive leagues. As children get older and the competition level rises, most leagues have separate boys' and girls' divisions.

are very low-pressure. Players get the opportunity to play a variety of positions and compete with (and against) their friends, while also giving them a chance to build their individual skills.

> **Yellow Card**
>
> The best part about rec leagues is the chance for kids to play a lot of positions. No child should always play goalie, for example, unless he specifically asks to play there all the time. Encourage your child to try a variety of positions while in rec leagues, so they get a better idea of what they like best.

AYSO and USYSA

The two main national organizations in youth soccer are the American Youth Soccer Organization (AYSO) and the United States Youth Soccer Association (USYSA), both of which run a variety of leagues throughout the country.

In some towns, both organizations have leagues; in other towns, only one does. AYSO leagues are run under the philosophy that every player plays, no matter what his or her skill might be. There aren't tryouts or cuts, and there is a strong emphasis on balancing teams and good sportsmanship. All the referees and coaches in AYSO are volunteers.

USYSA is the larger of the two organizations, and it affiliates with local rec leagues (where kids play against kids from their own town), as well as travel and select teams (which we'll cover later in this chapter).

> **Throw-Ins**
>
> If you want to contact either of the two main soccer organizations, here is their information:
>
> AYSO
> Phone: 1-800-872-2976
> www.soccer.org
>
> USYSA
> Phone: 1-800-4SOCCER
> www.usyouthsoccer.org

Playoff Time

If your rec league has a playoff bracket (in my town it was called the Pele Cup), there may be some changes in the intensity of the games when the postseason begins. Be prepared for this.

Although most leagues will continue to use the same playing-time requirements they did during the regular season (each player has to play at least one half of the game, for example), it's possible that the coaches may go strictly by the book and give some kids only the minimum. Instead of having games end in a tie, "the golden goal"—where the first goal scored in overtime wins—may be used.

Kids, too, may have different emotions about their introduction to "crunch-time" or may be nervous about making a mistake in a game where a loss means elimination. Be supportive and encouraging, and tell them to treat this game just like any other—there's no use getting anxious about a situation that can't be controlled.

The Differences in U6/U8 Leagues

At the youngest age levels, the mission of the league is for kids to learn teamwork and good sportsmanship, and to improve their soccer skills. That's why many younger leagues don't keep standings from week to week. At the end of the season, every kid gets a participation trophy or ribbon, with some coaches giving each player a specialized award (Most Improved, Best Effort, Hardest Shooter, etc.).

There are a few modifications that many U6/U8 leagues make that will be noticeable to you:

- ◆ Smaller field and goals
- ◆ Eight players on a side instead of 11
- ◆ Games broken into quarters instead of halves
- ◆ More instruction from referees (if an illegal throw-in is taken, for example)

Not every league makes every change at this particular age group (and some make them for even older kids). The point with all the modifications is to make it easier for young players to get plenty of time with the ball while at the same time making the game as fun as possible.

Travel Team

If your child is seeking an upgrade in competition on the soccer field, the travel team is the next step up. These leagues are typically composed of teams from nearby towns playing against each other at corresponding age groups (the Larchmont U10 team would play the Mamaroneck U10 team).

Some states have varying degrees of competition within the travel team structure; an "A" league might be the top division while the "B" league is a little less competitive. Check with your local soccer association to see what levels they offer.

Yellow Card

Joining a travel team may mean that your child won't be able to play with all his friends. This is something you should discuss with him before making the decision to leave the rec league and try out for the next level.

Whatever the level, in almost all cases playing for a travel team requires a tryout, an experience that most kids—and their parents—find at least a little nerve-wracking.

Trying Out for the Team ... and Making It

Most tryouts involve some short-sided games (say, five players against five players with tiny goals), some technical drills (dribbling through cones or markers), and scrimmaging. The overall key to making a good impression at any tryout is demonstrating confidence with the ball and sound decision-making skills.

Coaches want players who are comfortable on the field because they are the types of players who make their teammates better, too. What are some other tips to having a good tryout? Try to keep these in mind:

◆ **Arrive early.** Coaches running tryouts will be watching everything, even the warm-ups, so why not arrive at the field early and get a few touches on the ball with a friend or parent? That way, when everyone else is struggling to get loose, you'll already be comfortable with the ball.

◆ **Get involved.** Don't ever lay back in a tryout; aggression is what gets people noticed. This doesn't mean being reckless; it just means you should be making an effort to win the ball and then do something with it. If you're a defender, don't just take the ball away and pass it off to a midfielder; run up and support the attack. Do whatever you can to influence the game.

◆ **Talk.** Coaches want leaders on their teams, and most leaders open their mouths. You don't have to be friends with the players around you to communicate with them. Tell them if an opponent is approaching or which direction they should pass. Compliment and encourage good plays; call out moves that might be effective if a teammate has the ball. Constantly talking shows coaches that you're staying focused on the game.

◆ **Don't get down.** The best players are the ones who put their mistakes behind them immediately. If you lose the ball, hustle back and try to take it from the player who stole it from you. If you can't do that, make sure you're in a position to help play defense elsewhere. Just don't put your head down and sulk. That's the worst thing you can do and shows the coaches you have trouble bouncing back.

If you do all these things, will you be guaranteed to make the team? No, but it'll definitely enhance your chances. Most of all, be friendly, outgoing, and look as though you're having fun on the soccer field. That kind of positive attitude is a big attraction to a coach who is looking for players.

So How Much Travel Are We Talking About?

Congratulations! Your child made the team and now your family is preparing for the first season of travel soccer. What can you expect?

Commitments vary from team to team, but generally a travel team practices at least once or twice a week and has at least one game on the weekends. When I was playing, we would often practice Tuesday and Thursday evenings for about 60 to 90 minutes, then typically play our games on Sunday mornings.

What's that mean for parents? A lot of time in the car. Practices will be local, but even at the lowest travel levels there's going to be some driving to get to away games. Depending on the size of your league or county, it could be significant miles.

Make sure you're able to commit the time it'll take to get your child to everything he'll need to attend, and make sure he's ready to make that commitment, too. In addition to the typical weekly schedule, there will probably also be one or two tournaments each season.

 Yellow Card

Balancing time can be difficult for new travel team players. Weeknight practices plus schoolwork and other commitments may seem like too much. Help out by writing out a schedule for the week, with time for both homework and relaxation built in. Seeing it all on paper can make everything feel less overwhelming.

These events are often held during holiday weekends—Memorial Day, Columbus Day, and Labor Day are popular—so that can affect vacation plans, too. Some tournaments may be one-day, there-and-back events, but others may be out of town and require time and money to stay at hotels. Ask about any tournament plans at the beginning of the season so you'll have time to adjust your own schedule.

Cut Day

When I went through my first tryout for a travel team, I remember being so nervous when I came home and found a letter from the coach of the team addressed to me. When I opened it and found congratulations and a practice schedule for the season, I was flat-out giddy.

Unfortunately, it doesn't always work out. Not everyone makes the team and dealing with being cut is often a child's introduction to rejection. Will it happen again? Sure it will. But at that moment, there's nothing in the world that hurts more.

WELL DONE!

> Sometimes the best thing a parent can do is just follow the child's lead. If your daughter wants to dissect her tryout to figure out what she did wrong, you can listen; if she wants to vent, you can let her do that, too. If all she needs is a hug, you've got no problem providing that either. Just let her take the lead on how she deals with her disappointment.

In his book *101 Ways to Be a Terrific Sports Parent,* author Joel Fish says that, as a parent, there are a few things you should (and shouldn't) do to help your child through this situation:

- **Do** give a positive reality check, even before cut day comes down. If it's a long-shot to make the team, be realistic without being discouraging. Focus on effort, not outcome, and tell her you'll be proud of her no matter the result, so long as she does her absolute best.

- **Do** offer positive options. Let him know that if he wants to try out again next season, you'll work with him every Saturday to improve. Point out other alternatives, such as trying to play for a different team nearby or a lower-level league where he can do well and impress the coaches. If you make it clear that being cut isn't the end of the sports world, it may soften the blow.

- **Don't** make the child a victim. Saying things such as, "You got robbed!" or "The coach had something against you" will only add another layer of emotion.

- **Don't** deny the child's loss. If you say, "Who wants to be on the stupid soccer team anyway," you're diminishing the disappointment he's feeling. Who wants to be on the team? He did. Don't make him feel bad for wanting that.

Most coaches tell the players that were cut what they need to work on and the skills they should try to improve. If your child doesn't get that feedback from the coach, encourage him to reach out to the coach and ask. Doing so can only help at the next tryout, and will show the coach your child is genuinely interested in getting better.

Select/Premier Teams

The next step above the traditional travel program is select or premier teams, which typically draw players from a wide geographic area. Players don't have to be from a certain town; these teams are generally made up of the most talented players and play more intense schedules.

This means more practices, more tournaments, and very likely longer travel to play games against teams of similar talent level. Playing premier soccer is an even larger commitment, both for the player and his family.

Yellow Card

One thing to be aware of with select and premier teams is playing time. Talk with the coach to find out how he distributes minutes because there may be little value in being on the best team around if your child sees the field only rarely.

Knowing Whether Your Child Is Ready

There's no magic formula to determine whether your kid should make the jump to a premier team. If he has shown significant talent and doesn't mind dedicating a big part of his life to soccer, then he should go to a tryout and see what happens.

Know going in, however, that just because he dominates his current travel league doesn't mean that he'll necessarily be ready for the jump to premier. Skill levels vary widely from area to area, and as I said before, premier teams draw players from all over. Be prepared.

Also know that there will be sacrifices to play on a top-level premier team, especially as a child gets older (in the high school years).

Being able to play other sports becomes more difficult because balancing practice schedules and schoolwork can be cumbersome; something may have to give, and

Throw-Ins

Most select and premier teams take breaks during the high school season so that their players are still able to play for their school team. Training then resumes at a full schedule after the high school season is finished.

it might be basketball or baseball or some other sport your child has played all his life.

Faced with playing travel soccer and keeping his spot on the lacrosse team versus giving up lacrosse to join a select team may be a very tough decision. As a parent, you need to do your best to make sure he understands the ramifications of his choice.

Thinking About the Future

If you think there is a chance your child might be able to play soccer in college, playing on a premier team can be helpful because many of those clubs take part in "showcase tournaments" where college coaches scout potential players.

It's also worth knowing about a newer program recently started by U.S. Soccer called the Development Academy. A number of soccer clubs around the country are joining the Academy, which is organized nationally and will give players incredible exposure to top-level coaches.

There is no hard and fast rule about what age a player should begin playing premier soccer if she hopes to play in college (or professionally), but most coaches say that 16 years old is generally when players should be pointed in a particular direction.

Again, talk honestly with your child about what she wants to get from soccer. If she believes she's good enough to go far with it, there's no reason she shouldn't be playing in the highest level of competition possible.

The Least You Need to Know

- An instructional clinic is the best way to introduce young children to soccer. Your local JCC or YMCA probably offers one.

- The higher the level of play in a league, the greater the commitment a player (and his family) will have to make to the team.

- Tryouts can be wrenching experiences for both parents and children. Be positive and supportive.

- Playing for a premier or select team is a valuable way to increase exposure for players who have aspirations of playing in college and beyond.

Chapter 3

Dress For Success

In This Chapter

- ◆ Picking the right kind of cleats
- ◆ Why shinguards are important
- ◆ Discovering the different kinds of soccer balls
- ◆ Outfitting the goalie

Outfitting a soccer player is a relatively low-stress, low-cost proposition. Unlike football, there are no shoulder pads or helmets to try on. Soccer equipment—as with the game itself—is pretty simple.

Of course, kids always grow up fast, so keep that in mind when you're shopping for soccer gear. If your child is growing at a fast pace, maybe it's wise not to buy the most expensive products available. By the time you've finished paying for them, they might not fit your Pele-in-training anymore.

It's Gotta Be the Shoes

The most important piece of equipment each soccer player has is his shoes. Because soccer is played primarily on grass—which may or may not be wet on any given day—wearing regular sneakers puts a player at a huge disadvantage when he tries to turn quickly.

There are a wide variety of soccer shoes, and the goal should always be to pick a pair that offers the greatest comfort for the greatest value. Remember: almost everything a soccer player does on the field involves his feet. Without the right shoes, the game will feel a whole lot harder.

WELL DONE!

When you're taking your child to buy new cleats, make sure you bring along a pair of soccer socks to use when she's trying them on. If she usually wears two pairs of socks (a regular pair underneath her soccer socks, as some players do), then bring both so she'll be able to simulate how the cleats will feel on the field, as well as get the correct size.

Cleats (The Ones with Spikes)

If you pick up a standard soccer cleat and turn it over, you should see many rubber bumps protruding from the bottom; if you see any metal, you're probably looking at a baseball shoe. Either way, most youth leagues don't allow players to wear cleats with any metal on them.

Yellow Card

It's natural to just stuff your soccer cleats in a bag after the game, but a little maintenance will make them last a lot longer. Bang the mud off the bottom and run a cloth over them to get any dirt off the leather. Then stuff newspaper inside so the shoes hold their shape.

These basic rubber cleats are called "molded" cleats.

Cleats should fit snugly, with just enough room to wiggle your toes in the front. Unfortunately, buying cleats a size or two big in anticipation of a child "growing into them" is a bad idea. The whole purpose of wearing cleats is to provide stability and traction for the player; if she's swimming in her shoes, she'll be at a greater risk of hurting herself.

So suck it up and recognize that, with most kids, you'll probably be back in the store every season or two for new cleats.

It could be worse: you could be doing the same thing every winter with new hockey skates, which cost a lot more.

Turf Shoes (The Ones with Bumps)

There has been a significant increase in the number of soccer fields that utilize synthetic grass in recent years, so before buying cleats for your child it would be smart to investigate just what type of field he'll be playing most of his games on.

If it's FieldTurf or some other artificial surface, you might want to consider a shoe with smaller cleats that will be more comfortable. Don't be confused: this isn't the old-style Astroturf which is basically like a carpet with cement under it; these new surfaces often have composite rubber bases with fake grass on top of it, to give a more authentic feel.

Ask the coach or local soccer shop owner what he recommends for the specific surface in your town. As a general rule, if you're unsure of the best type of cleat to buy, go with a standard molded cleat, which should be fine to wear on almost any surface.

 Throw-Ins

Don't try talking about your "cleats" over in Europe; they're called "studs" there.

Beauty Is Shin Deep

Ever walk into a coffee table? Nothing hurts worse than a big welt on your shin, right? Now you know why shinguards are necessary equipment for soccer players. With all the kicking and flailing that goes on in a typical game, legs are perfect targets for an errant foot or two.

Some kids may not like the idea of wearing high socks over their shinguards, or even wearing shinguards at all. They may say it's dorky or it makes it harder for them to run. Tell them it doesn't matter. All leagues require players to wear shinguards and even if they didn't, you're putting yourself in a position to hurt yourself or someone else.

I've seen it a lot: the player not wearing shinguards at the beginning of the game is usually the one limping off at the end of it.

Leg Armor

How do you pick shinguards? The best way is to try them on and see if they cover your shins (complicated, right?). Some experts say you can measure from your knee to your ankle and then subtract an inch or so, but the best way is to go to a store and try a few pairs on with high socks on top of them, just as in a game.

Take a light jog around and see if the shinguards move around too much or if they rub or bite or otherwise feel uncomfortable. If not, take 'em.

WELL DONE!

As players get older or join more competitive teams, it may be worthwhile to get a more specialized shinguard for whatever position they play most often. Defenders often wear heavier, thicker shinguards for greater protection; forwards go for thinner shinguards because it gives them a lighter feel when they're running or trying to shoot.

Especially at younger ages, you don't need fancy, expensive shinguards. Most shinguards are made of plastic or foam padding and slide right onto your shin underneath your sock, or alternatively, have a little ankle brace attached that you put your foot into with a Velcro strap at the top to hold the guard in place. Again, spend 10 minutes in a store and find the one that feels the most comfortable.

Knee-High Socks

It's a good idea to have at least two pairs of soccer socks, if only because it's nice to have a dry pair available if one of them ends up getting soaked during a rainy game.

Soccer socks are advantageous to regular tube socks because they're typically softer and have more padding in the heel and toe areas, which can reduce rubbing against the cleats and make blisters less of a problem. Again, trying a few types of socks before settling on a brand makes it easier to figure out what's most comfortable.

Throw-Ins

When I was a teenager, my travel team went to Massachusetts for a weekend tournament. After the first day of games, we all gave our uniforms to one of the parents who was going to wash them. The next day, when we went to get our clean uniforms back, our white shirts and shorts were suddenly powder blue! The lesson? Soccer clothes, especially dark socks, can easily bleed in the laundry. (And yes, we played the last day of the tournament in our "new" colored uniforms).

Why do soccer players have to wear high socks? The main reason is that the socks cover the shinguards; this makes sure you're protected and keeps other players from being cut if an edge of shinguard plastic should end up protruding.

Shirts and Shorts

When you get above your feet and legs, the rest of a soccer uniform is pretty unimportant to actually playing the game. The major component to picking out a shirt and shorts is that the article of clothing be comfortable and allow the player freedom of movement.

Yellow Card

I can't stress enough how important it is to label every single piece of equipment you buy for your child. Put your name on everything. Shirts, shorts, socks, cleats (on the inside of the tongue), balls, water bottles—label it all. With a bunch of players running around, it's way too easy for things to get misplaced. An indelible marker can avoid a lot of confusion.

Soccer jerseys come in all shapes, sizes, and colors. Some have collars, others don't; some have stripes, others don't. Most shirts and shorts are made of some kind of blended material and are lightweight. Although basketball players often wear shorts that sag below their knees, that style hasn't really caught on in soccer, mostly because tripping and falling down isn't a very good strategy.

In most leagues, teams will issue matching uniforms. At higher levels, clubs have two uniforms—a light and dark one, with one worn for all home games and the other for games as the visiting team.

Spheres of Influence

Should you buy your child her own soccer ball? Let me say this in the most assertive way possible: *yes!*

Even though you need only one ball to play a game, every youth coach in the world wants each player to show up at practice (and even games) with his own ball. It just makes everything easier.

There are three sizes of soccer ball. The standard soccer ball used by older children and adults is called a Size 5 ball.

At some point, the soccer establishment decided that younger players should use a smaller ball, and that ball was called a Size 4 ball. It's mostly used by players aged 9 to 12.

WELL DONE!

Check the compression of the soccer ball every now and then to make sure it hasn't gone too soft. A good test to see if a ball is properly inflated is to hold it out in front of you at chest level and then drop it on the grass: it should bounce to about knee-level.

Not surprisingly, when kids began playing soccer at even younger ages, the Size 3 ball was created as well, though not every league uses Size 3s. If your child is starting soccer at a very young age, check with your local clinic or league to see what size ball they'll be using.

In case you're interested, a standard soccer ball (Size 5) has 32 panels, is 27–28 inches in diameter, and weighs 14–16 ounces.

Foul-Weather Friends

Soccer games can be—and often are—played in cold or rainy weather. Especially at older and more competitive levels, bad weather doesn't mean the game will be canceled. That means you need to be prepared.

I used to always carry a turtleneck in my bag in case of cold temperatures, and it's probably a good idea to have a pair of thin gloves, too. Dressing in layers is advisable, because then it's easy to remove a layer if you warm up during the game.

As for dealing with rain, there's no easy solution other than to have a few extras in your bag—extra socks, undershirt, and shorts. This way you can make a change at halftime and at least start the new half with a semi-dry feel.

Goalies: The Clowns of the Soccer Field

Goalies are different in many ways and the most noticeable—other than the whole "using the hands thing"—is that they dress in a completely distinct uniform. In fact, it's not a choice; the rules say they must look different than their teammates so that the referee will always be able to easily identify each team's goalie.

This means goalies can wear outrageously colorful jerseys if they so choose. The trend for goalie shirts now is less loud, but when I was a kid I had a goalie shirt that literally looked like someone had spilled three or four cans of paint on a red canvas and then put a collar and sleeves on it. Did I feel cool or what?

At the youngest age levels where several players may rotate in as the goalie, using a red "pinny" or vest over top the regular uniform is fine; if your child becomes a full-time goalie, however, it's worth investing in a couple of goalie jerseys. These will have padding on the elbows (to make diving more pleasant) and should fit loosely (but not be oversized), so that it's easy to move around.

Padded Pants

The biggest occupational hazard with being a goalie is the ever-present raspberry on both hips that comes with sliding to make saves. Fortunately, by wearing compression shorts (or "spandex") underneath your regular soccer shorts, you can insulate your legs a little from all the friction. Many companies even make a special goalie's compression short which has extra foam padding sewn into the hips.

Throw-Ins

It's always best to try on a piece of soccer equipment in the store to make sure the fit is correct, but there's no rule that says you have to pay your local store's price. Feel free to shop around for bargains, especially online. Here are a few soccer equipment websites:

www.eurosport.com

www.soccer.com

www.soccershop.com

Goalies are also allowed to wear long pants if they prefer, and there are several brands of goalie pants available. These are generally not too baggy and have knee and hip pads already sewn into them. If you play on fields that have bare goalmouths or rocks on the field, a pair of long pants can spare a lot of pain for a young keeper.

Sticky Fingers

In addition to the funny-looking jerseys and shorts, the thing that really makes goalies look clownish is those big, floppy gloves. Goalie gloves are designed to give the goalie a better grip on the ball, making it easier to catch.

The first set of gloves I ever had were basically nothing more than some nylon gloves with pieces of bumpy rubber sewn into the palm and fingers. For young goalies, that'll do fine.

As you get older, the options can quickly become overwhelming. As with everything else, choosing a glove mostly comes down to personal preference; some will fit you better, some will offer just the right amount of cushion. Goalie gloves can be expensive, so see if it's possible to try out a brand you're considering buying.

Whatever brand you end up with, treat the gloves well. Clean them off after games with a little dab of water and some paper towels, and keep them in their own little bag so that they don't get crushed or torn.

The Least You Need to Know

◆ The most basic kind of soccer shoe is the "molded," which has round rubber cleats on the bottom.

◆ Shinguards are the most important piece of equipment other than cleats, and should be worn at every practice and game.

◆ Every player should have his or her own soccer ball.

◆ Goalies have different needs: different jerseys and pants, and they get to wear gloves, too.

Chapter 4

Ready For Action

In This Chapter

- ◆ The object of the game
- ◆ What the markings on the field mean
- ◆ Understanding the different positions
- ◆ Changes made for the youngest players

A soccer game isn't a particularly complicated event—the field doesn't have yard lines or bases or dirt, the two halves are played without the clock visibly stopping or starting, and there isn't any kind of complex scoring system.

Although newcomers to soccer may find it confusing at first, soccer is really pretty easy to follow. Even though the pace and quality of skill level may change as players get older, the basics of the game itself are the same for 10-year-olds as they are in the MLS.

Chalk Outlines

A standard soccer field.

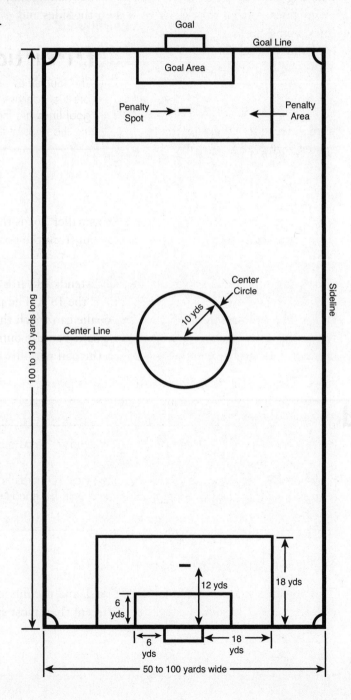

A soccer field is laid out on grass or another surface with chalk lines defining its boundaries. The field should be rectangular, with *touchlines*, or sidelines, setting the out of bounds on the sides and *goal lines*, or end lines, doing the same at the ends of the field. The field should always be longer than it is wide.

There should be a line striped across the middle of the field, with a circle drawn at the exact center of the field.

def•i•ni•tion

The **touchlines** on the field are the sidelines, whereas the **goal lines** are the lines defining the ends of the field.

What's with All the Boxes?

Near each goal there are two boxes. The smaller box is the *goal area*, which is a rectangle that extends 6 yards out from the goal line (it's sometimes called "the six").

The larger box is the *penalty area*, which extends 18 yards out from the goal line (the box is sometimes called "the 18"). The penalty area is the only area on the field where the goalie can touch the ball with his hands. This is why it's rare to see a goalie venture outside the penalty area—if he does, he can only touch the ball with his feet, just like everyone else.

def•i•ni•tion

The **goal area** which is a rectangle that extends 6 yards out from the goal line (it's sometimes called "the six").

The **penalty area** is the larger box and extends 18 yards from the goal line. The goalie is allowed to touch the ball with his hands inside the penalty area.

Falling In and Out of Bounds

The touchlines define the sides of the field, and the inbounds and out of bounds rules in soccer are a little different than most sports.

In football and basketball, for example, the line itself is out of bounds—if a wide receiver steps on the line after catching a pass, he's out of bounds. Same for a point guard in basketball.

In soccer, the line itself is inbounds. In fact, if any part of the ball is touching any part of the line, the ball is still in play. Only when the *entire ball goes over the entire line* is the ball considered out of bounds.

Spots and Hash Marks

Twelve yards from the center of each goal line is a dot (or, on some fields, a short line). This is called the penalty spot. This is where the always-dramatic penalty kicks are taken (see Chapter 5 for more on that).

You may also notice several hash marks on the goal line near the corner. These marks are drawn 10 yards from the corner and are used as a way to indicate where defenders are allowed to stand at certain points of the game (see "Corner Kicks" in Chapter 5).

Tickling the Twine

Each goal is 8 yards wide by 8 feet high. This is, all things considered, a very big goal (which is why it seems a little odd that there's so little scoring). The goal posts can be square or round, and there should be a net hanging off the back of the posts and crossbar.

Soccer goals are heavy. If you're asked to help move one, make sure there are enough people on the job (at least three or four people, preferably adults). The best way is to tip the goal forward (so the front is facing the ground) then pick it up at each end of the two posts and carry it that way. Then tip it back up at its new location.

> **Yellow Card**
>
> Some kids, especially those who have just gotten taller, may think it's fun to jump up and hang on the crossbar. This is incredibly dangerous. If you see any players doing this, make sure you step in and tell them to come down. Goals can tip over very easily and someone could get seriously hurt.

Watching the Watch

A professional soccer game is made up of two halves of 45 minutes apiece. In youth games, the time is modified depending on the age of the players. In the league I played in as a kid, 9- to 10-year-olds played 25-minute halves, 11- to 12-year-olds played 30, 13- to 14-year-olds played 35, and 15- to 19-year-olds played 40. Most adult leagues play the standard 45 minutes.

Although many stadiums will show the time on a scoreboard, the official time is kept on the field by the referee. Many stadiums will actually stop their scoreboard clock with two minutes left so that it's clear the referee is the one in charge of deciding when the game is over.

Also the referee does not "stop the clock" at any point during the game. Instead, he adds on time at the end of each half to make up for any time lost due to treatment of injuries, players wasting time, or anything else he deems necessary. This is called "added time," and, at high-level games, you may see an official on the sideline hold up a board indicating how many added minutes there will be at the end of the half or game.

In youth games, most coaches will have their own stopwatch running on the sideline so they'll have some idea of how much time is left. If you're watching your child play, you might want to do the same (or at least take note of the time when the game started and then follow from there). If you don't, there won't be an easy way to determine just how long a wait you've got until the break.

Parsing Positions

There are three basic types of positions in soccer (not including goalie), all of which have different general responsibilities. Especially at younger ages, most players will spend time at each one so that they get exposed to all aspects of the game. This is a good thing.

If your child is just getting into soccer, you should encourage him to give each position a fair try, if only because it'll make it easier to determine which one he enjoys the most. Sometimes kids surprise themselves—they may think they love one position but then do well at another and suddenly that is their favorite.

WELL DONE!

You never know when your child might be asked to play a new position. Even at older age levels, sometimes injuries create a situation where a forward needs to play fullback or vice versa. Encourage your child to work on all his skills, not just the ones he uses most. You never know when he might need to play somewhere new.

It's also important for kids (and parents) to realize that there are no hard and fast rules about positions in soccer. Unlike football, where a defensive lineman can never catch a pass, every player on the field in soccer can score a goal just as every player on the field can—and should—play defense.

Feisty Forwards

Forwards, sometimes called "strikers," are a team's attackers. They score the majority of the goals and spend much of the game in the opponent's half of the field so that they will be in position to receive passes near the goal.

What makes a good forward? Remember that there is no set requirement for any position, but forwards are often very fast, which allows them to race past defenders and find open space for a shot. Some forwards are also good dribblers and accurate shooters, the kind of players who can create their own scoring opportunities with the ball at their feet.

Some teams like to use taller players at forward—particularly thin, lanky players—because they have an advantage in heading lofted passes or high balls near the goal.

When forwards don't have the ball, they should be running into open space between defenders to make themselves available for a pass from a teammate. If the other team has the ball, forwards should be getting back on defense to help out, particularly if the other team's defenders have run up to join the attack.

Musical Midfielders

Midfielders are the go-betweens on the soccer field; they have to be involved in the offense and the defense. The best midfielders are soccer maestros, directing the play with passes and by communicating with their teammates. They are involved in everything.

One of my close friends was the center midfielder on our travel teams growing up and he was by far the best dribbler. That's a great skill for a midfielder to have, because he's often the one receiving a pass from a defender and then looking to give the ball to an attacker—the whole play flows through him.

Midfielders also need to be in great shape. Although every player on the field does a lot of running, midfielders do the most. Think about it: they have to sprint up to help the forwards, then sprint back to help on defense. Back and forth, back and forth—it's no wonder midfielders usually have the most tired legs after a game.

When they don't have the ball, midfielders should be either looking to get open to receive the ball or else looking at the play in front of them and calling out instructions to the teammate who does have the ball. When the opponents have the ball, midfielders are usually the first ones to try to challenge them and take the ball back.

> **Throw-Ins**
>
> Many of the so-called "best players in the world" are midfielders. Cristiano Ronaldo, who is a goal-scoring wizard for Manchester United in England, is a midfielder. So, too, is David Beckham, who is known for his bending shots and precise passes. Midfielders are always in the spotlight because they have the ability to affect the game at both ends of the field.

Most coaches make their most skilled players into midfielders because they are integral to a team's success. Midfielders are usually smart and savvy, the kind of player who sees the game well and is a natural leader.

Dominating Defenders

Defenders are usually known as fullbacks in soccer, and their main job is to help protect their team's goal. The prototypical defender is a big, strong, burly player who is able to muscle attackers off the ball and kick it long, high, and far down the field.

This type of fullback is effective, but is not the only kind of player that can be successful on defense. Any player that shows prowess at stealing the ball from opponents or intercepting passes is a prime candidate at fullback, as is any player who has a "nose for the ball" and goes after it aggressively. Loose balls in front of the goal are dangerous, so fullbacks need to be fearless in controlling the ball and kicking it away.

The majority of coaches put their weakest dribblers at fullback because there isn't much dribbling involved. When a fullback gets the ball, she should be looking to pass it to a midfielder or simply clear the ball out.

Differences for U6/U8 Players

Although young children seem to have unlimited energy, having them play a 90-minute game on a standard-size soccer field doesn't make much sense. Most leagues make some modifications to their games that involve the youngest players, changing the field dimensions and some of the rules. The changes vary from league to league, but here are some of the alterations you may see:

♦ **Smaller field:** Some leagues will turn one standard field into two smaller ones by going across the field in each half. Others will make the fields even smaller, turning one into four or six. Obviously the penalty area and other markings are proportionally smaller as well.

♦ **Smaller goals:** A "standard" smaller goal is 6 feet high by 18 feet wide, which gives younger goalies a fairer chance to make saves.

♦ **Fewer players:** Some leagues will make games as small as 4 vs. 4 (with no goalies). It's also common to see 8 vs. 8 (with goalies) before making the jump to the standard 11 vs. 11. This gives younger players more room to run and makes for less crowding around the ball.

◆ **Smaller ball:** A Size 3 ball is often used at the youngest age levels. It is lighter and easier for players to control.

Remember, the goal at the U6/U8 level is for kids to have fun, get some exercise, and get used to the idea of soccer. That's why most leagues don't keep standings for these teams, and why the most important part is making sure every player plays a significant amount of time each game. If children enjoy themselves at this age, there's a greater chance they'll want to stick with soccer as they get older.

The Least You Need to Know

◆ Although soccer might seem confusing at first, it's actually a pretty simple game to understand.

◆ The referee—not the scoreboard—is the official timekeeper during a game.

◆ The three basic positions (other than goalie) are forward, midfielder, and fullback.

◆ Most leagues will make modifications to the rules and field during games between the youngest-age players. These rules are designed to make the game more enjoyable.

Crime and Punishment: The Laws of the Game

Part 2 is designed to give you a quick primer on what is (and isn't) allowed during a game so you'll always understand what's happening when the referee blows his whistle.

Chapter 5 lays out the various fouls that players commit and explains the two types of free kicks that are awarded. Chapter 6 gets into discipline and discusses what it means when the referee shows a yellow or red card to a player (nothing good!).

A complicated law is made easy to understand in Chapter 7 when offside is covered, and Chapter 8 wraps up the part with a short explanation of the referee himself and some tips on the best ways for parents to deal with refs (hint: don't offer him your glasses!).

Chapter 5

Felonies and Misdemeanors

In This Chapter

- ◆ What players aren't allowed to do
- ◆ How direct and indirect kicks are different
- ◆ Why didn't the ref call that?
- ◆ What happens when the ball goes out of bounds

Soccer is a free-flowing game and even when the referee has to blow his whistle, there won't be a long-winded explanation of what foul or infraction was just called. The game simply starts back up again rather quickly.

So how do you know what just happened? Soccer's laws aren't that complex, so if you saw something that looked illegal—a push or a shove or a trip—it probably was. The beauty of soccer is that the game will keep moving: a foul is committed, the whistle blows, and the other team just takes the ball and puts it back in play. The action keeps on going.

Direct vs. Indirect

Anytime the game is stopped for any reason, a *restart* takes place to get the ball back in play. Restarts can take many forms, but two of the most common are the *indirect kick* and the *direct kick*.

Both are types of free kicks awarded to a team that has been fouled. The difference is that a team is allowed to score from a direct free kick (in other words, they can kick the ball directly into the other team's goal), while an indirect kick must be touched by at least two players (the player taking the kick and one other) before it goes into the goal.

Both types of free kicks are generally taken at the spot where the foul took place. The only exception is if a foul is committed in a team's own penalty area and results in a direct free kick (see "Penalty Kicks" later in this chapter).

On any free kick, the defending team must be at least 10 yards away from the ball and cannot come any closer until the ball is kicked.

def•i•ni•tion

A **restart** refers to a player putting the ball back into play after the game has been stopped. Two common restarts are the **direct kick**, which is a free kick that a player is allowed to score from; and an **indirect kick**, which means a second player must touch the ball before it can be shot into the goal.

What Causes a Direct Kick

Fouls that result in the other team getting a direct kick are the more serious or "major" fouls. If a referee sees a player commit one of these fouls, she will blow her whistle and point one arm toward the goal that the fouled team is attacking. That team then puts the ball down where the foul occurred and takes its kick.

The direct free kick fouls include …

- ◆ Kicking an opponent
- ◆ Pushing
- ◆ Tripping

- Jumping into an opponent (while trying for a header or otherwise)

- Charging an opponent (running into them)

- Holding (including grabbing an opponent's shirt or shorts)

- Tackling an opponent instead of the ball

- Touching the ball with hands (except for the goalie inside the penalty area)

There is no rule on how long the fouled team has to wait before taking its direct kick. If the team wants to take it right away, that's allowed. The only time a team has to wait for a whistle from the referee to take its direct kick is if the referee stops the game to move back defending players at least 10 yards. After counting out the appropriate distance, the referee will then blow the whistle and the fouled team can take its kick.

What Causes an Indirect Kick

The more minor infractions typically result in a team being given an indirect kick. You'll know that a kick is indirect because the referee will keep one arm raised straight up after blowing the whistle and signaling a direction. He'll only drop his arm after two players have touched the ball (remember, a team can't score straight from an indirect kick).

The fouls that result in an indirect kick include the following:

- Dangerous play (say, trying a high kick that comes near another player's face)

- Obstructing another player (i.e., running in front of that player just to keep him from getting where he wants to go)

- Being offside (explained in Chapter 7)

- Interfering with the goalie when she tries to throw or kick the ball after picking it up

- Touching the ball a second time after any kind of restart (in other words, a player can't put the ball back into play and then be the next player to touch it)

There are also two specific infractions that a goalie can commit that result in an indirect free kick:

- ◆ Taking more than six seconds to release the ball after making a save. If the goalie holds the ball longer than that, the referee will award the other team an indirect kick.

- ◆ Touching the ball with his hands after it has been passed to him or thrown to him by a teammate.

These are the only times a goalie isn't allowed to use his hands even if he is in the penalty area. He can play the ball with his feet, but if he uses his hands then the other team gets an indirect kick.

Throw-Ins

> Up until the early 1990s, the goalie was allowed to pick up the ball inside the penalty area whenever he wanted. This made it easier for a team that was leading to kill time. Near the end of the game, they'd simply pass the ball back to the goalie, who would then pick it up and punt it away. By changing the rule, soccer officials were hoping to encourage more attacking play.

As with direct kicks, indirect kicks are taken at the spot of the foul (even inside the penalty area). The only exception is if a direct kick is awarded inside a defending team's goal area; then the kick is taken on the edge of the goal area.

What happens if a team shoots an indirect kick straight into the goal? Because two players must touch the ball before a goal is scored from an indirect kick, the ball is considered to have simply gone over the goal line and out of bounds, so the defending team gets a goal kick.

Playing "Advantage"

You saw a foul committed. It was obvious to everyone, including the sleeping dog lying on the sideline. But the referee doesn't blow her whistle. Why?

Instead of assuming she's in need of glasses, watch to see if she raised both arms in front of her and called out, "Play on!" If she did, she applied *advantage*, which means choosing not to call a foul because doing so would help the team that fouled.

Think of it this way: let's say you've got the ball and are about to pass it to a teammate who could have a chance to shoot. Just as you do, I slide in and trip you. That's a foul, but wouldn't you be mad if the referee blew her whistle and gave you a free kick instead of allowing your teammate to take the pass and score?

That's the premise of the advantage—making sure that calling a foul doesn't actually hurt the team that has been fouled.

def•i•ni•tion

If a referee decides that a team who has been fouled would benefit more from not having the foul called—i.e., the ball rolls to another player who can continue attacking—he can invoke the **advantage** and not stop the game for the foul.

Penalty Kicks

If a direct free kick foul is committed inside a team's own penalty area, the other team is awarded a *penalty kick*, which is a one-on-one shot taken from the penalty spot. You'll see in a minute why goalies hate when this happens.

The ball is placed on the spot (located just 12 yards from the goal line) and the shooting team selects one player to take the kick. The goalie stands on the goal line and everyone else must clear out of the penalty area until after the kick is taken.

def•i•ni•tion

When a player commits a direct-kick foul inside his own penalty area, the fouled team is awarded a **penalty kick**. This is a one-on-one shot taken from just 12 yards away.

The referee blows the whistle and the shooter takes his shot. Because the goalie is the only one who can stop the shot (and the shot is taken from so close), it's not surprising that at higher age levels, penalty kicks are scored a very, very high percentage of the time.

Throw-Ins

If the ball goes out of bounds over one of the sidelines, the team that *did not* touch it last gets to put the ball back into play with a *throw-in*, which is taken from behind the line at the spot where the ball went out.

def•i•ni•tion

If the ball goes out of bounds over the sideline, then a **throw-in** is awarded to the team who did not touch it last. If the ball goes over the end line, a **goal kick** is given if the attacking team touched it last and a **corner kick** is given if the defending team had the final touch.

Throw-ins are the only time that field players are allowed to touch the ball with their hands. If this seems strange to you, you're not alone. Why a throw-in instead of a kick-in? Beats me. It's just the way it's always been.

There are two keys to executing a legal throw-in. Here's what you have to do:

1. **Keep both feet on the ground.** This means you're not allowed to jump, skip, or hop when you throw the ball in. You are allowed to run up to the sideline before you throw the ball, but when the ball leaves your hands, some part of both feet must be on the ground. Some players will do a run-up and then drag one foot as they throw; others just stand flat-footed. Either way is fine.

2. **Bring both hands behind your head.** In other words, no one-handed throws; no sideways throws; no underhand throws. You must use two hands equally (so no big spinning throws) and bring the ball back behind your head and then forward, following through as much as you want.

Especially at younger ages, this is not the easiest move to pull off. The laws of the game say that if a throw is taken improperly (one foot is off the ground, for example) then the other team is awarded a throw-in.

This is the proper set-up for a throw-in. Notice how both feet are on the ground and both hands are behind the head.

In younger leagues, there may be a local rule that gives players a second chance to try the throw-in as a way of making sure every player learns the right way to do it.

Goal Kicks

Not all shots are on target, so when an attacking team kicks the ball over the goal line, the defending team is awarded a *goal kick*. The ball can be placed anywhere inside the goal area and any player (including the goalie) can take the kick.

A goal kick must leave the penalty area; if it doesn't and a player on the defending team touches it, the attacking team is awarded an indirect kick. If an attacking player touches the ball before it leaves the penalty area, the kick is simply retaken.

Corner Kicks

If the ball goes over the goal line and was last touched by a player on the defending team, a *corner kick* is given to the attacking team. These can be valuable scoring opportunities.

The ball is placed in the corner circle on the side of the goal where the ball went out and, as with free kicks, the defense must stand at least 10 yards away from the ball.

A goal can be scored directly from a corner kick (though it's tough to do), and most teams take the opportunity to kick the ball from the corner, right in front of the goal, in hopes that one of their players will be able to knock it into the goal.

Kickoffs

This is used at the start of the game, at the beginning of the second half (or overtime), and after a goal has been scored.

There isn't much to it: the ball is placed at the center of the field, and the team taking the *kickoff* puts it into play. The only rules are that all players must be on their side of the field, the defending team's players must be outside the center circle, and the ball must go forward. Also the player kicking off can't touch the ball again until another player has touched it.

The most common kickoff method is for two players on the team kicking off to stand next to each other. One player taps the ball forward a few inches and the other kicks it backward to a midfielder, who then dribbles the ball or passes it.

def•i•ni•tion

At the beginning of a half and after a goal, teams use a **kickoff** from the center circle to put the ball back into play. If the game is ever stopped for any unusual reason (such as an injury), a **drop ball** is held between one player from each team.

Drop Ball

Sometimes a game has to be stopped for an unusual reason. A dog ran onto the field, maybe, or a player is injured and needs to be checked on. If something similar to this happens, the referee will restart the game with a *drop ball*.

If a drop ball is necessary, one player from each team comes forward and the referee drops the ball between them. The players must wait until the ball touches the ground before trying to play it.

Although it's unusual, a player is allowed to score directly from either a drop ball or a kickoff.

The Least You Need to Know

♦ Soccer games don't have extended stoppages after fouls are committed; the fouled team takes a free kick and the game resumes.

♦ A direct free kick is awarded for most of the serious fouls and an indirect free kick is given for more minor infractions.

♦ Throw-ins must be taken with both feet on the ground and both hands bringing the ball behind the head.

♦ If the game is stopped for any unusual reason, a drop ball is used to restart it.

Chapter 6

Color Coding

In This Chapter

- ◆ The basics of soccer's discipline system
- ◆ Knowing each player's "personal traffic light"
- ◆ What causes a player to receive a yellow or red card
- ◆ How misbehaving coaches and parents are dealt with

As in life, not everyone plays by the rules during a soccer game. Inevitably there will be kids who are bigger or stronger and like to throw their weight around (literally and figuratively), or a player who is just a little too aggressive for his own good.

Fortunately, soccer has a pretty simple discipline system. It's strict enough to cut off foul play quickly, but flexible enough that a referee—at least a good one—can adjust his standards based on the age and playing level of the players. Oh, and there are no little yellow handkerchiefs being tossed around as in American football; instead, soccer uses cards (much more refined, right?).

Yellow Cards: Proceed with Caution

Imagine that each of the players begins the game with a green light on their very own personal traffic signal. They can go anywhere, running (or driving) freely.

There are certain things that a player can do, however, that will cause the referee to show them a *yellow card*. This is also called being "cautioned," and it means exactly what it sounds like. The player's personal traffic light is essentially being switched to yellow: they've got to be more careful now, because they've been warned and the next step is a red card which means—you guessed it—they're going to have to stop playing (and thus, have their traffic light switched to red).

def•i•ni•tion

A **yellow card** is how referees give players a warning. Two yellow cards in the same game and the player will be ejected.

Warning Signs

Most fouls are just fouls—a free kick is awarded and the team that was fouled puts the ball back into play. Simple.

Sometimes, however, a player will do something that the referee feels is worthy of a yellow card. The most common causes for receiving a yellow card are the following:

- **Committing "unsporting behavior."** This could mean a particularly harsh foul, such as a bad trip from behind or jumping up and grabbing the ball with a hand. It's basically a catch-all phrase for things a player might do that aren't just your run-of-the-mill fouls.

- **Constantly fouling.** If a player keeps tripping other players or is pushing opponents over and over, the referee can show a yellow card. Although each individual foul might not be that bad, the collection of fouls by the same player isn't allowed.

- **Dissent.** This doesn't mean a player can't ever speak to the referee. It just means that players aren't allowed to repeatedly question fouls or yell at the official. Every referee has her own tolerance for questions and comments, so the best thing players can do is to generally keep their criticisms to themselves.

♦ **Intentionally delaying the other team's restart.** The beauty of soccer is its constant motion, so if a player doesn't allow the opponent to take a free kick (or corner kick or other restart) by running in front of the ball or kicking it away after a foul has been called, then he will get a yellow card. Most coaches tell their players, "leave the ball alone" after a whistle has gone; if it's the other team's kick, just let them get the ball and put it back in play.

> **Yellow Card**
>
> Time-wasting is a big sticking point for referees because it just isn't fair to the other team. If a player takes forever before taking a goal kick or throw-in and is clearly trying to waste time because his team is winning and the game is almost over, the referee will almost surely step in and give him a yellow card.

In any of these instances, the referee will stop play and call the player over. Then he'll write their number down on his scoresheet and show them a yellow card before allowing the game to resume.

What Happens Afterward

In many leagues, a player who gets a yellow card has to be substituted and, even if it's not required, most coaches will replace the player at least for a little while. This "cooling-off" period is a good idea because the player has to be careful in how she plays the rest of the game. One more yellow card and she'll also get a red—which means an ejection.

It's hard for players to hold back when they're playing, but yellow-carded players have to watch themselves. Slide tackles should be done with care (because a poorly timed one can often result in a yellow card) and talking back to the referee is definitely a no-no. A yellow card is a warning and players who get one should play accordingly.

Verbal Caveats

Sometimes you'll see two players "getting in each other's face" or otherwise acting foolish. The referee may not want to give a yellow card but does want to head off anything unruly, so he'll give them both a verbal warning.

This isn't anything official but it should be taken seriously. If a referee stops to talk to a player, it probably means he'll be watching that player closely to make sure the player changes his behavior. If he doesn't, you can bet the yellow card will be coming out quickly.

Red Cards: Thanks for Stopping By

Red cards aren't good—not for players, not for teams, and not for referees. No one ever wants to throw a player out of the game, but rules are rules and there are certain things that players do which are grounds for an immediate ejection (without getting shown a yellow card).

def•i•ni•tion

A **red card** is how the referee indicates he is ejecting a player. The player must leave the field immediately and his team cannot substitute for him.

Some of the things that a player can get a red card for are obvious, but there are a few fouls a player might not expect to be ejected for committing. A smart coach will go over these situations so that players are sure to avoid them.

The Seven Deadly Sins

Unlike "Soccer's Sacred Seven" basics, which we went over in Chapter 1, this list of seven isn't positive. Referees have a list of seven reasons they can give a player a red card, and they include …

1. **Using foul language or gestures.** How this is enforced depends a lot on the age of the players, but the spirit of the rule is designed to keep the game clean.

2. **Spitting at another person.** Pretty self-explanatory, no?

3. **Violent conduct.** This covers hitting, punching, kicking, and everything of that ilk.

4. **Serious foul play.** A particularly reckless or dangerous foul, such as sliding into an opponent with cleats aimed toward their knee.

5. **Denying an obvious goal-scoring opportunity by using hands.** A shot is going in the goal and you knock it out with your hand. If you're not the goalie, you may have saved a goal but you'll have given up a penalty kick and earned a red card to boot.

6. **Denying an obvious goal-scoring opportunity with a foul.** If a player is on a breakaway and you trip him from behind, you've denied your opponent a goal-scoring opportunity with a foul. Red card.

7. **Getting a second yellow card.** No three strikes here. If a player does something that's worthy of a yellow card and she's already received one, she'll get a red card.

Regardless of the reason for the red card, the procedure is the same: the referee stops the game, calls the player over, and writes his number down on his scoresheet. He then shows the red card and the player has to leave the field immediately.

What Happens Afterward

The worst part about a red card isn't what it does to the player who receives it (though being ejected is pretty bad); it's that the player's team has to play a man short for the rest of the game.

In other words, if Little Teddy gets a red card with 15 minutes to go in the first half, his team has to play with 10 players (instead of 11) for the next 15 minutes *and* the entire second half. Definitely not good.

What happens if a goalie gets a red card? In that case, a substitute goalie is allowed to come on, but the team must choose a different player to come off the field so that they are still playing with only 10 players.

Suspensions

In most leagues, a player that gets a red card will have to sit out at least one additional game and, depending on what he did to get the card, possibly more.

During one of my high school seasons a good friend of mine got a red card in the first round and, because we still managed to win, he was suspended for the next game, too. It was agony, he said, having to watch us play without him and when we lost it hurt even more. Coaches and parents should tell their players to think about the consequences of their actions before they do something on the field that they'll only end up regretting.

Wait, You Get a Red Card for That?

Within the seven "deadly sins" for which players can get a red card are two fouls that might not seem so bad yet are penalized with ejection, so they're worth a little more explanation.

"Denying an obvious goal-scoring opportunity with a handball" actually seems like a pretty smart idea, doesn't it? If a defender is standing near the goal line and sees that his goalie can't make the save, isn't it better to stop the certain goal and give the other team a penalty kick instead? At least the goalie would have a chance then.

Not surprisingly, soccer wants to discourage this kind of play so it makes the consequence more severe. Yes, you've saved a goal (at least for the moment) but now you're costing yourself a suspension and your team one player on the field for the rest of the game.

Throw-Ins

In one of the last travel-team games I played as a teenager, I was playing goalie and a forward on the other team stole the ball and came in on a breakaway against me.

I came out toward him and lunged to try and get the ball, but succeeded only in tripping him as he tried to dribble past me. He went down, the referee blew his whistle, and I knew what was coming next: a red card and the end of my day. Sigh.

The same principal applies to "denying an obvious goal-scoring opportunity with a foul." This only applies to a player breaking in alone against the goalie. If there is another defender between the attacker and the goalie, it isn't an "obvious" scoring chance so there's no red card for a foul. If the attacker is on a breakaway, however, and a player takes him down, you can bet a red card will be coming out.

Hit the Road, Jack

If you've ever spent any time around youth sports of any kind, you already know that most of the time it's not the kids that need the disciplining. Parents and coaches can really run the gamut from supportive and encouraging to downright disastrous when it comes to how they act on the sidelines.

Some leagues allow referees to show yellow and red cards to coaches, in addition to players, while others simply have their referees deal with unruly coaches and fans without cards. Either way, all parents and coaches should know that there can be consequences if they feel the need to "express themselves" to the referee in an ugly manner.

How a Coach Can Get Sent to the Parking Lot

Most coaches know the right way to coach and treat their players, the opponents, and the referee with respect. Unfortunately, there are always a few who don't.

If a coach is constantly berating the referee, calling her names, or otherwise using foul language, the referee will likely hold up the game the next time the ball goes out of bounds and have a short conversation with the coach. That's the warning.

Should the harassment continue, the referee is in her rights to eject the coach. In most leagues, that means the coach has to leave the field—he's not allowed to stay and watch and he's not allowed to talk to the players anymore. Most of the time, that means he's going to be spending the next hour or so just sitting in his car.

The worst part is that if there's no assistant coach present, then the game may have to be forfeited (because a team can't play without a coach). All the more reason for coaches to be a good example for their players and treat the refs with respect.

How a Fan Can Get Sent to the Parking Lot

I played in a game once where the father of one player on the other team just would not keep his mouth shut. From the first minute of the game he was all over everyone—his son, other players, and especially the referee.

This kept up for a little while, until the Disastrous Dad used some choice language to describe a call the referee made, screaming so loudly that I'll bet people on the nearby highway heard him. That was enough for the ref.

WELL DONE!

The best thing for parents on the sidelines to do is focus on encouraging the players and leave the referee out of their comments entirely. It sets the best example for the kids and keeps the attention on the game—where it should be.

For those parents who think the refereeing in their area is so bad, here's an idea: check out Chapter 8 to see how to become a certified ref yourself.

He went over to that team's coach and told him that if the coach didn't have the parent leave the field immediately, the game would be forfeited. He said it quickly, simply, and then stood there until the coach—somewhat timidly, if I recall—relayed the news.

Disastrous Dad didn't know what to do. The game was stopped and everyone was looking at him. Finally, he just sort of shuffled off to his car to wait for his son, and the game resumed (at a much more pleasant volume).

What the ref did was standard procedure for that league, and most leagues don't want referees confronting fans directly. That doesn't mean they can't deal with inappropriate parents all the same. If Disastrous Dad hadn't left the field, he would have cost his son's team the game.

The Least You Need to Know

- ◆ Soccer uses a two-card system to deal with discipline: yellow cards are warnings, red cards are ejections.

- ◆ Red cards are a double-whammy; not only is the player ejected, but his team has to play with one less player (10 versus 11) for the rest of the game.

- ◆ Most players know that egregious actions such as punching or hitting an opponent result in a red card, but other red-card fouls—such as using your hands to stop a shot that's going into the goal—might not be so obvious.

- ◆ Coaches and parents can be subject to discipline from the referee, too.

7

Understanding Offside (a.k.a. "Rocket Science")

In This Chapter

- Simplifying a tricky rule
- The reasoning behind offside
- Applying the rule in game situations
- A short pop quiz

Every sport has one rule that's just hard. Baseball has the infield-fly rule, football has pass interference, and soccer has offside.

There are plenty of coaches, players, and fans who don't fully understand the offside rule and probably even some referees, too. It's just one of those rules that's tough to get your head around—but when you do, you'll probably look back and wonder what all the fuss was about.

A Hard Rule Made Easy

Here is the simplest way to explain the basic offside rule: a player is in an offside position if, at the moment a teammate plays the ball, he is closer to the other team's goal than both the ball *and* two opponents (99 percent of the time, the opposing goalie will count as one of the two). If a player is called offside, the opposing team gets an indirect free kick from the spot where the offside player was standing.

Confused already? Take a look at the following diagram:

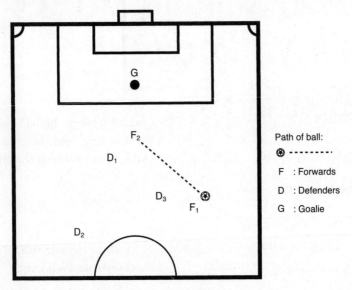

Player F₂ is in an offside position.

Player F₁ has the ball and passes it to Player F₂, who has only the goalie in front of him. That's only one opponent, not two, so Player F₂ is offside. If Player F₂ had backed up so he was even with Player D₁, then he would have been onside.

Remember, too, that we said the determination of whether someone is offside is made *at the time the ball is played*—not when the player receives it. Check out this diagram:

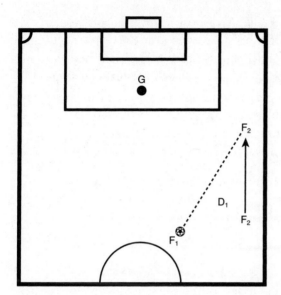

Player F₂ is not in an offside position.

See how this time Player F_2 started in a position where he had two defenders (the goalie and Player D_1) in front of him, and then ran past D_1 after the ball had been played? Because he was onside at the time the ball was passed, there is no offside called.

So What's the Point?

Most soccer fans that are trying to understand the offside rule have a common reaction: why the heck does this crazy rule even exist?

It's a fair question, and knowing the answer might help you understand the rule itself. The basic premise of the offside rule is to eliminate goal-hanging.

WELL DONE! If your daughter is a forward who is constantly getting called offside, mention the "circular run" to her. This is a basic move that many high-level players use to avoid offside: basically, they constantly loop around the fullbacks, waiting for a teammate to pass the ball to them. This way, they never stop moving (so they're always ready to catch up to the ball) but they'll also be onside because they'll be just in front of the defenders.

After all, with 11 players on the field, most teams probably wouldn't mind having one of their forwards stationed near their opponent's goal. That way, anytime a midfielder or forward gets the ball, they can boot a long pass in the direction of that forward and the team has a good scoring chance.

The only way to stop the tactic would be to have one defender assigned to that forward, who would then have to spend the whole game just hanging around his own goal. Definitely no fun.

So to make sure this scenario never happens, the all-knowing soccer gods came up with an offside rule that basically allows forwards to only go as far up the field as the defense lets them.

The "Offside Trap"

Sometimes a team will make it part of their defensive strategy to catch the opponents offside. This is called the *offside trap*, and is accomplished by having the team's defenders constantly running up toward the midfield line.

def•i•ni•tion

The **offside trap** is a tactic that skilled teams sometimes use in which the defenders constantly run forward, so as to intentionally put the opposing forwards offside.

Remember, forwards are offside if they don't have two defenders between them and the goal line, so if the fullbacks keep moving up the field, the forwards have to run back along with them. Otherwise, they'll be offside when a teammate passes to them.

This is a very tricky tactic for a team to try and it can have disastrous results if one fullback is slow running up—usually it ends up with a forward having a breakaway and a great chance to score.

Yellow Card

A team that is using the "offside trap" should always be on the lookout for players making long runs from the midfield. An attacking team will often try to have a midfielder time it just right so that he will be running past the fullbacks who are running up, just as the ball is passed over the top of them. Because the fullbacks are running away from the ball at that point, the forward is onside and has an open shot on goal.

Get Out of Jail Free

Just because a player is in an offside position doesn't mean that the referee will actually blow his whistle and call offside. The rule was designed to only penalize players who are affecting the play, so very often you'll see a play such as this one:

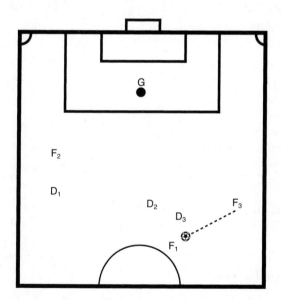

The "F team" isn't penalized for offside because the offside player isn't involved in the play.

If Player F_1 had passed the ball to F_2, then the referee would have definitely called offside. Because the pass went to F_3, however, and F_2 wasn't involved in the play, no call is made.

There are also a few situations in which a player has "offside immunity." In other words, a player can never be called offside if ...

1. She receives the ball directly from a throw-in.

2. She receives the ball directly from a goal kick.

3. She receives the ball directly from a corner kick.

4. She receives the ball directly from a player on the opposing team (so, if an opposing player passes the ball backward in your direction because she thinks you're on her team, you can't be called offside).

5. She is in her own half of the field.

It's important to know that these exceptions apply only to a player who gets the ball directly. If Player A throws the ball in to Player B and Player B then passes it to Player C who is in an offside position, the referee will call offside. The throw-in exception only applies if Player A throws the ball in to Player C directly.

Let's Get Specific

Even if you understand the basic premise of the offside rule, there's still the matter of actually recognizing its use during play. Inevitably, even the most knowledgeable soccer parents will be watching their son's team play, see a big scoring chance develop, and then yell out, "Noooooo!" when the referee blows a whistle for offside.

There are a few plays that often leave fans wondering, "Why was that offside?" Let's go over a few.

Rebounds from a Shot On Goal

Here's the situation: Jeff is dribbling down the right side of the field and when he gets near the penalty area, he tries a shot that the goalie dives to stop. The ball rebounds from the goalie toward Matt, who had been running ahead of the play on the opposite side of the field and immediately kicks the ball in the goal. When Jeff took his shot, only the goalie was between Matt and the goal line.

Does the goal count or is Matt offside?

The answer is that the goal doesn't count and Matt should be called for offside. Remember, offside is determined by where the player was when the ball was played. In this case, the ball was played when Jeff took the shot. Because Matt wasn't involved in the play at first, no offside needed to be called and if Jeff's shot had gone in, it would have been a goal.

After Matt became involved in the play, however, the referee has to call him for being offside. It doesn't matter that the ball came off the goalie because the moment of judgment for the offside had already happened (at Jeff's shot).

Think you got it? Try another one.

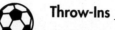 **Throw-Ins**

A player can be "involved in the play" and not actually touch the ball. I've seen referees (correctly) call offside in situations where a forward has simply stood in front of the goalie, making it difficult for him to see an incoming shot. Even though the offside player doesn't touch the ball, he's clearly involved and offside is the right call.

Shots Off the Post

This time it's Maggie running down the field. She jukes right, goes left, and rips a shot that slams into the corner of the goal where the right post and crossbar meet. The ball bounces up in the air and Marian, who had sprinted behind the defenders before Maggie shot, is standing right near the post and heads the ball directly into the goal. She immediately runs off and celebrates while the defending team looks to the referee hopefully.

What's the call?

If you said no goal and a whistle for offside, you're right. The thinking is basically the same as the previous situation. The ball hitting the post doesn't "reset" the fact that Marian was standing in an offside position when Maggie shot the ball, and as soon as the ball came toward her, she was involved in the play. That means she's offside.

A Sneaky Pass

The Turkeys are losing by a goal late in the game, so they've pushed all their players, including the fullbacks, up into the Chickens' half of the field. Suddenly, one of the Chickens' halfbacks named Larry steals the ball and kicks it long down the field.

His teammate, Jerry, had been standing just inside the halfway line, with only the Turkeys' goalie between him and the goal. As soon as Larry kicks the ball, Jerry runs after it, goes in, and scores. Should he be called for offside?

Not this time. Remember what the offside "immunities" are from earlier in this chapter? One of them was that a player can't be called for offside if he's in his own half of the field. Because Jerry was "just inside the halfway line" at the moment Larry kicked the ball, it doesn't matter that there was only one defender (the goalie) ahead of him. If he's in his own half when the ball is kicked, he's onside and his game-sealing goal absolutely counts.

Pop Quiz

The average soccer parent has little or no knowledge of how the offside rule is called, so by simply reading this chapter you're already way ahead of the curve.

How well do you know soccer's toughest rule? Let's try a little pop quiz to find out. In each of the three situations, consider the circumstances and then decide whether the referee should call offside. Answers are at the end.

Question #1

The goalie takes a goal kick and summons the strongest kick he's ever had, booting the ball way past the center line and directly to a forward on his team that has been standing beyond the second-to-last defender. The forward takes one dribble and shoots the ball in the goal. Offside or not offside?

Question #2

A player has the ball on the right side of the field when he looks up and realizes a teammate of his has already broken past the last fullback on the opposite side of the field. The player with the ball hits a lofted pass to his teammate. Offside or not offside?

Question #3

Two fullbacks have been passing the ball back and forth to each other. On one of the passes, one of the fullbacks mis-hits the ball and it goes directly to a forward on the other team, who had been trailing behind the play and has no one between him and the goal but the goalie. The forward turns around, runs in, and scores. Offside or not offside?

Quiz Answers

Here's the breakdown to the quiz:

1. **Not offside.** Remember, receiving the ball directly from a goal kick is one of those times when "offside immunity" applies.

2. **Offside.** This is the most basic offside situation. If Player F_1 had seen F_2 a little earlier, he might have been able to pass him the ball before he ran past the fullbacks.

3. **Not offside.** Offside is only enforced when the ball is played by a teammate, not an opponent. Player F_1 isn't penalized for the defender's bad pass.

Did you get all three correct? If you did, you're definitely the offside authority on your sideline and should feel free to answer the questions of all the other parents who are wondering about that last call.

The Least You Need to Know

- ◆ Offside is the trickiest rule in soccer but that doesn't mean the average fan can't fully understand it.

- The basic offside rule is that a player can't be closer to the other team's goal than both the ball and two defenders (with the goalie counting as one).

- The main reason for the offside rule is to discourage teams from goal-hanging.

- If the ball goes to a player directly from a goal kick, corner kick, or throw-in, no offside can be called.

Chapter 8

Men in Black

In This Chapter

- ◆ What soccer referees do
- ◆ How to recognize the signals
- ◆ The best way to approach a referee with a question
- ◆ How to join the whistle club

Nobody likes referees, or at least it feels that way a lot of the time if you happen to be one. Making everyone on both teams happy is a virtual pipe dream; in fact, the joke goes that referees consider it a good day if both teams are equally unhappy at the end of the game because it probably means they called a fair one.

Truth is, most referees don't officiate games for the money or because they're on some kind of power trip. They're out there because they love the game and love being around it. Does that mean they're always above reproach? It doesn't. But it does mean they're people, just like you and everyone else on the sidelines. Think about that the next time you're ready to scream out something nasty.

The Whistle-Blower

In most youth games, there will be one referee. He calls fouls, keeps the time of the game, records goals, and signals when teams are allowed to make substitutions.

> **Throw-Ins**
>
> The referee always wants to be near enough to the ball to see what's happening, but not so close that he becomes an obstruction. So what happens if the ball hits the referee? Absolutely nothing. The referee is treated as "in play" and the players should continue playing normally.

The goal of the referee is, literally, to stay out of the way and protect the players from hurting each other. The best days for a referee are the ones where the players are the focus and no one really notices him. That's the ideal.

In some states and leagues, especially as players get older, there may be three officials at each game. One of them is the referee, who runs on the field and has a whistle. The other two are assistant referees (colloquially called "linesmen"), who have flags and work on the sidelines.

Why Does He Wear Yellow?

The stereotype of officials in all sports is that they're the ones wearing black (or black-and-white stripes). That isn't the case in soccer.

Although you may still see some referees wearing black shirts, the new official uniform is a yellow shirt. The United States Soccer Federation (USSF) has changed shirt designs a few times over the past decade or two, so now you might see yellow shirts, blue shirts, black shirts, red shirts, or even green shirts on referees, most of which will have some sort of pinstriped pattern.

What's That Patch All About?

Most referees will have a patch over their chest pocket. If it has the current year on it, it means that the referee passed a rules test and is certified by the USSF for that year.

Some referees, usually younger ones, may have a purple patch which means they're called an "associate referee," which basically just means they're a beginning ref. On the other end of the spectrum, you might notice a referee at a professional match wearing a white patch; this means he's a FIFA referee, which is the highest level and makes him eligible to work international matches such as the World Cup.

The Flag Bearers

If you're fortunate enough to live in an area where there are enough officials for each game to have a referee and two assistants working, be thankful—it's not the norm, especially in youth matches.

WELL DONE!

One of the main reasons cited by young referees who give up their whistles is that dealing with abusive parents is so demoralizing. It's pretty hard for leagues to cultivate better officials if young people interested in learning are run off before they even get started.

If you're a parent at a game with a younger official, take a moment and tell him or her after the game that you appreciate what they're doing. Trust me: it'll make a difference.

Many leagues will have a more experienced referee work as the "middle," or the ref who runs on the field and uses his whistle to call fouls, while younger referees serve as the assistants.

The assistants move up and down one half of each sideline on opposite sides of the field. They have prescribed duties and do not use a whistle, instead signaling to the referee with flags.

What They Call

Assistant referees are responsible for watching their side of the field. Specifically, they're looking out for the following:

- ◆ When the ball goes out of bounds
- ◆ Offside

◆ Fouls or misconduct that the referee can't see

◆ Shots that cross the goal line only briefly or other controversial goal/no-goal decisions

The assistants also help the referee manage the game by telling players to move back 10 yards on free kicks, organizing substations, and being a back-up timer and scorekeeper in case the referee makes a mistake.

An assistant primarily communicates with the referee by using her flag. She will raise it high to indicate offside and wait for the referee to blow the whistle and make the call; she will indicate which team gets to throw the ball in by pointing toward the goal that team is attacking; she will point toward the goal area to indicate a goal kick should be taken.

Although the referee typically will follow the calls indicated by the assistant, he isn't required to do so. The referee is the final authority and sometimes he may overrule the assistant and make a different call. His call is the one that stands.

What They Don't Call

Assistant referees don't have whistles and they're not in the middle of the play, so they don't make foul calls in the middle of the field or issue yellow and red cards. They're there to help the referee, not make her life more difficult.

That said, don't think that just because one player spit on another player behind the referee's back, there won't be consequences. If an assistant referee saw the spitting, he'll signal to the referee, call him over, and tell him what happened; then the referee will show a red card to the offending player and eject him.

The Sign Language of Soccer

As far as signals go, soccer referees have it pretty easy. Unlike football, where even the most rabid fans might not be able to identify the signal for, say, clipping, soccer refs keep it simple.

When a referee calls a foul, she simply blows her whistle and points one arm toward the goal the fouled team is attacking. That means that team has been awarded a free kick.

No identification of the foul itself is required, though some referees may call out what happened ("Holding the shirt!") or even do a quick signal of explanation (such as mimicking a push).

That's it though—the team who was fouled puts the ball down, takes its free kick, and play resumes. No microphone, no drawn-out descriptions of the penalty. Just a whistle and a point in one direction, and the ball starts moving again.

If a referee has awarded an indirect kick (as he would for offside), he'll put one arm straight up in the air. This is the signal that a kick is indirect, and the referee will keep it there until two players have touched the ball.

Yellow Card

Before you go crazy because Little Cleo was tripped in the middle of the field and the ref didn't blow his whistle, remember the advantage clause in the rules: if the ball rolls to a teammate of the player fouled, the referee may decide to let play continue. In this case, look for the referee to hold both hands out in front of him and yell, "Play on!"

Why does he do that? Remember that an indirect kick can't be shot straight into the goal, so the ref keeps his arm up until a second player touches it because that way if the ball goes into the goal before he drops his arm, everyone will know that the goal doesn't count.

The rest of the soccer signals are self-evident: to signal a corner kick, the referee points to the corner; a goal kick, he points to the goal area; a penalty kick, he points to the penalty spot. You get the idea.

The only signal that deviates is the one for a goal. It would be confusing to point at the goal (because that looks as though it's the one for a goal kick), so the referee points to the center circle instead.

Referees Have Feelings, Too

Dealing with referees during a game can be a challenge because every ref—as with every person—is different. Some are chatty and friendly, others are gruff. Some may welcome questions about the rules or situations in the game, others may not want to talk at all.

As I said before, the best advice for players, coaches, and fans is to ignore the referee—just focus on the game itself. But if you feel as though you absolutely *have* to talk to the ref for some reason, there are definitely some things to keep in mind before making your case.

How a Player Should Approach the Ref

Each team has at least one captain, and referees are typically more receptive if the captain is the one who asks for a quick word.

> **Throw-Ins**
>
> One time I was refereeing a game and noticed one team was missing a player who had been suspended after receiving a red card the week before. I asked the coach what had happened, and he sighed. "He called the referee a bad word," the coach said. "He actually did it in Spanish but the referee could understand it anyway and gave him the red card."
>
> I laughed and told the coach that most referees—especially at the higher levels—are taught curse words in several different languages so they're able to understand exactly what a player is saying about them. "Ohhh—I didn't know that," the coach said, before adding, "I guess my player didn't know that either."

Captain or otherwise, however, no referee—or official in any sport—likes to be "shown up" by a player. This means no jumping up and down, no screaming and yelling, no waving of the arms in all directions. That just embarrasses the ref and makes it much, much harder for a player to get her point across.

Wait until the ball goes out of play or there's a break in the action, and quietly ask the referee for a moment. Keep the tone calm and use a question: "Ref, number 3 seems to be grabbing my shirt a lot. Can you take a look for that the next time?"

How a Coach Should Approach the Ref

If you're coaching your child's team or even just helping out as an assistant coach, you need to be conscious of the fact that you're setting an example for the players. If you're calling the referee names or screaming, they'll think that it's okay for them to do, too.

If there's something you think the referee isn't aware of, wait until a stoppage of play—perhaps when another player's injury is being treated or, better yet, at halftime—and try to have the conversation away from the players and fans, if possible.

This lets the referee know you don't want to make a spectacle of talking to him and just want to let him know about something you think is happening. At the very least, he'll respect you for taking that approach and make an effort to understand what you're asking.

How a Parent Should Approach the Ref

Most parents think the referee has it in for their child and his team, especially if things aren't going well that day. It's natural.

Even so, the best thing parents can do is leave the referee out of their in-game yelling. Shout for your child or his teammates, but shrieking at the ref just makes you look like a whiner.

If something comes up during the game that you have a genuine question about—not just a "Why can't you open your eyes, ref?" kind of question—then the best way to talk with the ref is to wait until after the game, when you can have a normal conversation with him.

As I said at the start of this chapter, most referees love soccer and are happy to talk about the rules with an interested fan or parent. If you treat the referee with respect, he'll assuredly give it back to you.

Earning Your Stripes

One of the most common responses referees give when parents or coaches are berating them is to say something such as, "If you think the refereeing around here is so bad, why don't you sign up for the rules course yourself?" It's a good response and sometimes it even inspires the complainer to do just that.

WELL DONE! If you're looking to get involved in refereeing, here are a few websites that will get you started:

- www.ussoccer.com/referees/index.jsp.html (the starting point for referee hopefuls)
- www.officialsports.com (for uniforms)
- www.asktheref.com (great for rules discussions)

Becoming a referee is a great way to learn more about the game and stay involved with it, wherever you live and however old you (or your kids) are. Refereeing is also a great way to get plenty of exercise and get paid a little side money while you're doing it.

The first step is to sign up for an entry-level referee course. The course will teach you the intricacies of soccer's rules, as well as proper mechanics and how to manage a game.

Typically given during the course of several days or nights, the course will have a classroom element as well as work on the field. It then culminates in a written test: pass the test and you will be certified to referee.

After you've got your referee patch, ask your local soccer league to put you on their list of available officials. Most assignors are always looking for more referees and will be happy to give you games to work.

You'll have to take a refresher test to maintain your certification from year to year, and you can also seek to move up to higher levels of officiating by asking to be assigned to more advanced games. Either way, you can be certain that you'll have a greater appreciation for the referees working your child's game because you'll know just how hard a job they actually have.

The Least You Need to Know

◆ The referee's job is to call fouls, keep the game moving and, most important, protect the players.

◆ Assistant referees primarily watch for offside, out of bounds, and fouls the referee can't see.

◆ The best way to approach referees is with common courtesy: screaming, yelling, and jumping around is a surefire way to be ignored.

◆ Becoming a referee isn't a hard process and is a great way to get exercise, make some extra money, and stay close to the game.

Part 3

Practice Makes Perfect

Now that you understand the basics of how the game is played, figuring out how to play it is the next step. Learning soccer skills isn't difficult—as with everything else, it just takes some getting used to.

There are chapters in this part for each skill: Chapter 9 deals with controlling the ball, Chapter 10 is about dribbling, Chapter 11 covers passing, Chapter 12 is everything you need to know about shooting, and Chapter 13 handles how to play goalie. Each skill chapter has a variety of drills and games that will help players practice effectively. Some drills and games will be more effective than others, but the point to remember is that repetition matters. Whatever a player's age, the more he practices a soccer skill, the better he'll be.

Chapter 9

Controlling Your Own Destiny

In This Chapter

- ◆ What parts of your body you can use to trap
- ◆ How to utilize "give"
- ◆ The keys to juggling the ball
- ◆ Why trapping sets up everything else

Controlling a soccer ball looks as though it ought to be pretty easy. The ball is a nice medium size—not too big or too small—and it's not particularly hard or soft, either. Getting it under control shouldn't be that tough, right?

Truth is, trapping—which is the soccer term for "controlling the ball"—really isn't all that difficult. The basic skills are simple enough, and learning the more advanced nuances won't be overwhelming either. The key is just getting used to using everything but your hands to bring the ball under your command. When your body is comfortable with that concept, trapping really is a breeze.

Big-Game Trapper

As with just about everything else in soccer, your feet are the most common tools when it comes to trapping. Whether the ball is rolling, bouncing, or flying at you, the option to trap it with your foot is always there.

The thing to keep in mind when you're trapping with your foot—or any other body part—is the idea of *give*. To successfully control the ball, your foot must give as it makes contact; if you hold your foot stiff, the ball will ricochet away from you instead of falling softly in front of you.

def•i•ni•tion

When players talk about **give** in soccer, they're talking about cushioning the ball as it comes to them. Regardless of whether they're trapping with their foot, chest, or leg, they're doing their best to give the ball a soft landing—just as a pillow gives when you drop your head on to it.

Give is an important concept regardless of which body part you're using to trap the ball, but particularly when you're doing one of the two main foot traps.

The Inside (and Outside) of the Foot Trap

The most basic option for trapping is to turn your foot sideways and use the inside of it to receive the ball. This technique is most often used to receive passes that are rolling toward you, and is the simplest trapping technique. You can also use the inside of the foot for controlling skipping or bouncing balls.

To trap with the inside of the foot, first set your nontrapping foot at an angle; if it's pointed straight ahead, it's hard to open up your trapping leg to receive the ball. Then raise your trapping foot up so that it'll contact the ball in its center. This is important—you always want to aim for the center of the ball because if you are off the mark, the ball will either go under your foot (too high), pop up in the air (too low), or spin away (off to either side).

Again, you want to remember to give with the ball, allowing it to hit softly against your foot instead of bouncing hard.

Sometimes, you may find it more convenient to use the outside of your foot to trap the ball (if you are standing sideways and the ball is coming from that direction, for example). If that happens, the principles are basically the same; you want a little give to your foot so the ball bounces off the outside of it softly, and then you can make a decision on what to do next.

The Instep Trap

The instep is the top of your foot, the area where the laces on your cleat can be found. To successfully trap the ball here, you've got to lift your foot in the air and point your toe straight out, forming a tiny basket with your foot into which the ball can drop. This is the best way to trap balls that are coming from above you and are dropping fast.

Figuring out exactly the right place for your toes can be an issue; if you turn them up, the basket your foot makes looks a little deeper and wider, but you run the risk of the ball deflecting off the point and shooting away. If you push your toes down, it's harder to control the ball on your laces because the basket is a little shallower.

Yellow Card

The instep trap can be effective, particularly for balls coming at you on a shallow arc—say, from a popped-up header. There is a little danger in using the instep trap too often, though, because it leaves your foot exposed to an opponent trying to aggressively steal the ball. If you're not careful, you could end up with someone else's cleat stepping on the top of your foot. Ouch!

The best approach is to keep your toes—and your whole foot—loose, with the toes pointed naturally (probably just slightly descending), and then pretend your foot is a baseball glove that will catch the ball, making sure to use plenty of give with your knee and ankle. The ball should land right in front of you.

The Sole Trap

This is the simplest and most difficult trap to pull off all at the same time. How is that possible? Think of it this way: if the ball is just rolling slowly toward you, it's no big deal to lift your foot and simply put it on top of the ball to stop it. That's a sole trap—easy.

But now picture a long punt from the goalie coming in your direction and you're going to try to step on top of the ball again to control it. Doesn't that seem a little tougher?

In general, it's best to stick to sole trapping in the easy scenarios. If the ball is moving at a comfortable speed and you can just put your foot on it, go for it. You've got control.

Judging when to stamp down on a harder-moving ball takes more practice, and it can have some embarrassing—and painful—results if you misstep or trip over the ball.

If you're determined to use the sole trap, make it your goal to contact the ball just as it hits the ground. Too soon and you'll step into it, knocking it away; too late, and it'll bounce up into you. If you time it right, though, and step on it just as it lands, you'll pin it against the ground and have perfect control.

Thunder Thighs

Trapping with your thighs is the preferred way to deal with balls that are coming at you on a higher arc. These can be short chips, punts from the goalkeeper, or long passes from a player all the way across the field. Basically, if the ball is in the air and a foot trap would be too difficult to pull off, a thigh trap might be your best bet.

The general idea with a thigh trap is similar to the instep trap; you want to give the ball a soft landing and cradle it briefly before it falls at your feet. This is helped by the fact that thighs are fleshier than feet: much of the cushion is already built in.

Catching with Your Legs

Raise your right foot up high enough that your leg is parallel to the ground. You want to trap a ball about halfway down the front of your thigh. If you contact the ball much closer to your knee, it will probably shoot away from you; if you do it much closer to your stomach, it may catch your hip (and also bounce away) or your groin (less bouncing, more pain). In other words, the middle of your leg is ideal.

Try to imagine your leg as a baseball glove that is catching a soft fly ball.

Imagine that baseball glove again, but this time it's on your thigh. The same principles apply here: when the ball is coming, anticipate its contact and try to give it a soft landing so you can control it.

Bring It Up, Bring It Down

One key I always try to remember with trapping is the concept of rhythm. Smoothness is important and herky-jerky motions almost always result in the ball bouncing away.

With thigh trapping, I try to think of a Slinky. I know it sounds weird, but if you drop a Slinky, it looks tall as all the coils extend, but then it compresses as it hits the ground—and that's basically what a good thigh trapper will do.

If the ball is coming toward you in the air, it doesn't do any good to just raise your leg up and hold it there—for one thing, you can't move around to adjust to the ball's flight, and for another, you'll almost certainly stiffen your leg up, making your muscles tight and increasing the likelihood of a hard ricochet.

Instead, track the ball as best you can, move to where you think it's going to come down, and as it gets closer, raise your leg up to catch it then fluidly bring your leg down for control. Up then down. Up then down. If you do it right, the ball will follow your leg to the ground, and you'll be ready to pass, dribble, or shoot.

The Treasure Chest

The chest trap might be the toughest one to learn, if only because it's hard not to want to get your hands involved which, obviously, isn't legal in soccer.

> **Throw-Ins**
>
> The best chest-trappers are the ones who seem to literally catch the ball on their torso and then drop it at their feet. If you watch professionals, you'll see them barely break stride when they chest-trap; they can do it so smoothly that the ball simply falls right into their stride and they just start dribbling.

Still, a mastered chest trap can be valuable because you can literally push the ball in whatever direction you want, making it easy to trap the ball on the run.

Make a Heart Pocket

By now you've figured out that the overriding factor in all traps is giving the ball a pocket in which to land; it's the same with the chest. This time, you want to think of it as a "Heart Pocket," though that doesn't mean you necessarily need to trap the ball on the left side of your chest every time.

In fact, the standard chest trap should be targeted in the middle of your chest. The best times to try and use one side or the other of your chest are if you're hoping to trap the ball and then turn in a particular direction. If that's the case, trapping the ball on the left side (and then turning left, or vice versa) is the best choice. Wherever you have the ball hit you, make sure to keep your arms extended away from your body (for better balance) and watch the ball all the way into your chest.

From Push to Pull

The mechanism for getting "give" on a chest trap is similar to the up-down of the thigh trap, except this time it's more of a push-pull.

This time, the two-step process goes like this: when the ball is coming toward you, *push* your chest out slightly to greet it, and then *pull* it back in as the ball makes contact. Sound familiar? It's the same as every other type of trap—you're making a virtual basket for the ball that will allow it to land softly on you instead of bouncing away.

Yellow Card

Obviously the natural impulse is to arch your back slightly before a chest trap and that's the right thing to do—to a degree. You don't want to over-arch though, because that's when the ball will start bouncing off your chest and then over your shoulder, making it impossible to control.

You just want a slight arch; enough to open up your chest to the ball, but not so much that you feel a strain in your lower back. If you get a twinge down there—or the ball is constantly rocketing over you when you try to chest trap—it probably means you're over-arching.

The best way to chest trap is to remember the push-pull; push your chest out to greet the ball, then pull it back just as the ball hits you to cushion the blow. The ball should drop right at your feet.

Trust me: if you use the push-pull, 99 percent of the balls you try to trap won't hurt you or knock the wind out of you. The ball isn't that hard and your chest is strong enough to take it. I promise.

Circus Jugglers

Juggling is a great way to develop trapping ability because it's done by getting all parts of your body involved. Although juggling doesn't often get used in a game, there are moments when a good juggler can incorporate a juggling skill to give him an advantage.

Imagine this: the ball is coming down toward you from a goal kick and you're going to thigh trap it. You do your up-and-down technique, but this time, instead of just having the ball drop to the ground, you use your instep to flick it to the side where you then run over and start dribbling. By combining two traps—and, thus, using a juggling move—you've put yourself in a better position on the field.

You'll see players working on juggling all the time—before a game, on the sidelines when they're not playing, or even just on a slow afternoon.

def•i•ni•tion

Juggling means keeping the ball in the air using your feet, legs, torso, and head— basically any part of your body that's legal for use during a game.

 Throw-Ins

The world record for juggling is held by Martinho Eduardo Orige, a Brazilian who juggled a regulation soccer ball for 19 hours, 30 minutes in 2003.

It's a great way to perfect the trapping technique and you'll quickly see a difference in how confident you are with trapping during the game.

Games for U6/U8 Players

Working on trapping alone isn't much fun, so the best thing to do with younger players is to combine it with something else: either another soccer skill such as passing, dribbling, or shooting, or another sport— such as the Touchdown game in the next section—to keep it interesting.

Touchdown!

This is a great way to practice trapping but also make the kids feel as though they're the next Randy Moss or Jerry Rice. Instead of just tossing the ball in the air having them trap it, set up like a quarterback and have them "go out for a pass." They run to the "end zone," you toss them the ball, and if they're able to control it, they've scored a touchdown (which means they get to do their own touchdown dance). Keep track of how many TDs each player scores and, as they get better, progress backward until they're catching "the long bomb."

Hangman

You remember this classic car-ride game, don't you? Try to guess a word, letter-by-letter, and every time you guess a letter that isn't in the word, a body part gets drawn—guess too many wrong letters, and you'll end up with the noose around your neck.

This is a similar game. Each player has a partner who is standing a few yards away from him. One player tosses the ball to the other player, who has to trap it with a particular part of the body. If the player traps it, he gets to go on to the next part of the body; if the ball bounces away, that part of the body has to be used on the next toss.

In the beginning, keep it simple: two foot traps, two thigh traps, and a chest trap. First player to get through all of them wins, the others are "hangmen." As players get better, you can make the types of traps more challenging (has to be the left foot, for example) or increase the distance of the tosses.

Water Balloon Toss

This is a take on the popular barbecue game and is particularly good for use on a hot day. Again, have each player with a partner, but this time have them start just a few feet from each other. One player tosses the ball to the other softly and the other must control it.

If he does, each player takes one step backward. Then the second player tosses the ball back to the first, and he traps it. If he does, another step back. If a trap is missed, the pair has to go back to the beginning (where they were only a few feet apart) and may be subject to a squirt from the water bottle! Winners are the first group to successfully make it 10 steps back from where they started.

Shooting Gallery

Developing the instincts to use the correct part of the body to trap the ball takes time, but this drill will help hone that skill. Set up five large Hula hoops on the ground (or use cones or string if you don't have hoops) with a few yards between them. This is the "range."

Each player steps into the first hoop and receives a ball tossed to him; if he controls it inside the hoop, he jumps to the next one where another ball is tossed to him. If he can make it through all five, he's gotten through the shooting gallery and gets to be one of the tossers. The key is to keep the game going quickly and vary where the balls go—some at the chest, some at the feet. As the kids improve, keep increasing the pace.

Games and Drills for U10/U12 Players

Trapping is something that can always be improved, and as players get older it's a skill that is incorporated into almost any other practice drill. Still, it's worth making control a main focus occasionally, so here are a few games and drills that will really sharpen your control.

The Square

For this drill, you'll want four players to set up in the shape of a square (each player is a side); a fifth player is the defender who goes in the middle of them. The goal is for the four players to keep possession of the ball by passing it quickly around the square with this stipulation: they can't pass it across the middle.

WELL DONE!

Remember to stress communication skills in this drill. Even though the passing options are limited for each player, you still want everyone to get into the habit of calling out their location to the player with the ball. The more that kind of talking is practiced, the more it will show up in games.

By following this rule, the players are forced to learn how to control the ball quickly, look up, and make a quick decision. Because they can't use the long pass, they're also forced to keep moving when they're away from the ball (up and down their side of the square) so as to create a safe passing lane for their teammate to use.

Jump Ball

Give each player a number and then put the odd numbers in a line on one side of a 20×20-yard grid, the evens in a line on the other. Call out two numbers—one odd and one even—and those two players must run out into the middle, where you've tossed a ball into the air at one of them. That player must control the ball first, and then dribble past the other player.

His team gets one point if he successfully traps it, and a bonus point if he gets to his opponents' side of the grid with the ball. The winning team is the first to 15.

Check-Out/Check-In

Set up a 15×15-yard square with cones, and put one player on each side of the square. Two other players (A and B) go in the middle.

Give the ball to one of the players on the outside. Player A runs away from the player with the ball, before quickly checking back toward him so he can receive a pass; Player B should quickly close Player A down defensively, and Player A responds by passing the ball to another one of the players on the outside. He then repeats the check-out, check-in routine so he can receive another pass.

Do this four times each, and then change players in the middle. After a few turns in the middle, each player will have improved their ability to receive a pass at their feet while on the move, and also be better at trapping under pressure.

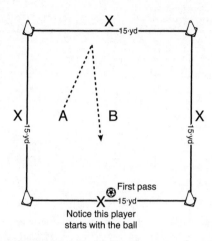

Players around the grid can pass to each other while Player A in the middle is trying to make space to receive a pass, but Player B cannot steal a pass from them; he's only allowed to take the ball after Player A has possession.

3 vs. 2 Forever

This is a good game for practicing trapping, shooting, and quick decision-making. Set up two goals about 30 yards apart and put two players in front of each, with three other players in the middle of the field.

The three players in the middle take the ball and pass it back and forth as they go toward one goal while the defenders try to steal the ball. If the attackers get a shot off, the player that shoots it turns around and goes with the two defenders in the other direction, and they try to score on the pair of defenders in front of the other goal. If a defender succeeds in taking the ball, he and his defensive partner join the player who lost the ball when going on the attack. The 3 on 2s continue in this way—back and forth—for 10 minutes.

Simple, right? The only catch is that each player is allowed no more than three touches on the ball at any one time. Ideally, that's one touch to trap, one dribble, then a pass or a shot!

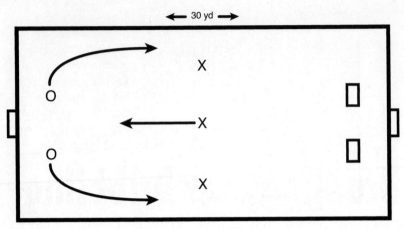

The key to this drill is to keep it moving quickly. As soon as a shot is taken or the ball is stolen, the next group of three should start passing the ball and moving toward the opposite goal.

The Least You Need to Know

◆ You can use any part of your body to trap the ball (other than your hands or arms), but the most popular traps are with your feet, thighs, or chest.

◆ The key with any trap is to give the ball a little cushion when it hits you, so it'll drop softly instead of bouncing away.

◆ If you're having trouble trapping, imagine a baseball glove on whatever part of the body you're using. Then try to see the ball landing softly in that glove as you make your next trap.

◆ A trap always comes before something else—a pass, a shot, or a dribble. A clean trap makes it easier for you to make your next move.

Chapter 10

Drooling over Dribbling

In This Chapter

- ◆ Keeping control of the ball
- ◆ Making correct decisions
- ◆ Using both feet
- ◆ Practice makes perfect

You've got the ball. Then they've got it. You've got it back again. But now they've stolen it once more.

Soccer isn't like football, basketball, baseball, or sports where possession of the ball is pretty clearly defined. In soccer, possession is fluid, changing all the time as the ball goes from one team to the other. Keeping control is hard, so the best teams—and the best players—are the ones that are comfortable with the ball at their feet. That's why dribbling is a crucial skill to master.

Inside, Outside, All Around

Dribbling in soccer means moving the ball around the field with your feet, and the key to being a successful dribbler is getting used to the idea that every part of both feet is involved in the process. This isn't like bouncing a basketball where the sides and back of your hand aren't particularly useful; in soccer, you want to use everything: inside and outside of the foot, instep, back of your heel on occasion, bottom of the foot, and yes, even the toe (though not as often as you might think).

Start by just rolling the ball around on your foot. Touch it with each part of both feet. Push it a few feet away, and then roll it back with your sole. Before you even get into moving with the ball, just get used to touching it while standing still. You can even try some juggling if you want—anything to make you feel a little more familiar with the ball at your feet. Confidence is critical to keeping control.

Running with the Ball

This is the bread-and-butter of dribbling, the way you move the ball around the field during the game (in combination with passing). Running with the ball doesn't mean that you literally have it at your feet the whole time, it just means that you have it close enough to make a move or change direction.

Sometimes that'll mean pushing it one way, sometimes that'll mean pulling it in another direction or stopping it entirely; the important part is that you've got the ball near enough to your feet to make those choices.

How do you do that? Think of it this way: the slower you're running, the closer you should keep the ball to your feet; the faster you're running, the further you can afford to let the ball get away from your feet.

The best dribblers I've ever seen are the ones who are able to integrate their touches into their running strides. That might sound hard to do, but it's easier if you use the outside of your foot to push the ball out in front of you—as you're rushing up the sideline, for example—then use the inside of your feet to bring the ball back closer when you need to slow down. Then you can decide which way you want to go next.

Yellow Card _____

Using your toe during dribbling can be helpful, but should be done sparingly because it's typically much more difficult to control. Because the toe is smaller than the instep or inside of your foot, you've got to be more precise with your touches: toe the ball a little below its equator and it'll pop up in the air and bounce away. Toe it too high and you might roll over it. There are times when the toe is useful, but as you're learning to dribble it's probably better to focus on the bigger parts of your foot first.

Seeing the Field

Dribbling—as with most things in sports—would be a whole lot easier if there was no one else on the field to bother you. Alas, there are 21 other players out there, too, so you can't fall into your own little dribbling world after you get the ball. You've got to keep your head up so you can see where your teammates are (so you can pass), where the goal is (so you can shoot), and where your opponents are (so you can avoid smacking into them).

There's no substitute for practice when it comes to mastering this skill. The only way you'll ever trust yourself to dribble the ball without constantly staring at it is to just do it. That's why you'll hear most coaches constantly calling out "Head up! Head up!" during dribbling drills. The sooner a player learns how to move the ball without looking down, the better off he'll be.

Is there a secret to doing it well? Not really. If you watch professional players, you'll see their heads bobbing a little as they move with the ball. They're mostly keeping their eyes up at the field, while occasionally stealing glances down to make sure the ball is still there. That's what you want to do: spend most of your time with your head up except for the occasional peek down, as opposed to doing the exact opposite.

Remember the Balance Beam

Did you ever take gymnastics as a kid? I did, and I always loved trying to make it across the balance beam. It's hard to do, but one of the ways to make it easier is to keep your knees bent and your body weight centered. If you stayed centered, you could probably make your way across the beam; if you shifted your weight to the side, you probably were seconds away from proving—yet again—just how gravity really works.

WELL DONE! Another similarity to the balance beam in dribbling is the value of keeping your arms out. The best players don't dribble with their arms at their sides—they keep them slightly raised, elbows bent. This helps them stay balanced but also allows them to feel when an opponent is coming closer to them—and gives them a subtle way of keeping the defender at arm's length.

The same principles of balance apply to dribbling. Keeping control of the ball is nearly impossible with stiff legs and an uneven posture. You want to be in an athletic position, with your chest over your feet—centered. Otherwise, your body will be going in several different directions and you'll be faking yourself out, instead of the defenders.

Big Dribbles, Little Dribbles

Dribbling is really nothing more than pushing and pulling the ball with your feet. Sometimes you push or pull hard, other times you push or pull soft. When some people think of dribbling they just imagine a player batting the ball back and forth between the insides of his feet—and that's a good way to build up confidence touching the ball. But the reality is that players don't spend much time during a game moving the ball in that fashion.

def•i•ni•tion

A **cut-back** is a dribbling move where a player suddenly stops his motion and quickly turns back in a different direction.

You also don't necessarily have to be going forward all the time when you're dribbling. Sometimes you'll be making a *cut-back* or turning with the ball, and sometimes you'll be moving parallel to the goal, which can help open up the field and give you more passing targets.

The key with the cut-back is to make the move quickly and change direction sharply. It doesn't matter which part of your foot you use to turn, so long as you don't do it slowly. Being fast is what makes the cut-back work.

The key with dribbling is to have a goal in mind—and not necessarily the one at the end of the field. Dribbling means keeping control, and keeping control is a big part of how a team wins.

Open-Field Dribbling

So you've trapped the ball, have it safely at your feet, and you've got your head up. There's loads of green grass in front of you, just begging you to push forward. What do you do?

First, you've got to know your limits. Space on a soccer field is always changing, so a 20-yard gap can quickly shrink to half that if one defender changes direction. That's why it's important to make your first touch on the ball a good one. Don't boot the ball way out in front of you and expect to catch up—that's a sure way to give the ball back to the opponents.

Instead, give the ball a comfortable push ahead with the outside of your right foot as part of your first stride forward. If the space is still there, do the same with your left foot on the next stride or two. You're moving fast, yes, but not out of control—you can always put your foot on the ball if you need to change direction.

Dribbling in Traffic

Most of the time, there are going to be people around you when you have the ball—and if there aren't, there probably will be pretty quickly. Figuring out how to move without losing the ball is one of soccer's toughest skills.

In these situations, you'll want to keep the ball close. If a defender is right up against you, you'll pretty much have a foot on the ball at all times, rolling it away from him. This is when you'll be using every part of your foot; use the outside to push it to the side, the inside to pull it across, and the sole to drag it away.

There's no one move that works every time you're stuck in soccer gridlock, but one thing to keep in mind is the importance of *shielding* the ball.

def•i•ni•tion

Shielding is when a player uses his body to block an opponent from getting at the ball.

There are certain things you're not allowed to do—such as extending your arms all the way out and purposely pushing defenders away—but you can, and should, turn your body in such a way that your back and legs keep your opponents from being able to poke the ball away from you. If you succeed at shielding, you'll be able to look up and pick where you want to move the ball next.

You're not allowed to push the opponent with your arms, but using your body to shield the ball is perfectly legal—and a very effective move to master.

Keys to Success

Much of being a good dribbler comes with repetition. If you're the kind of person who doesn't worry about what the neighbors say, try dribbling the ball around the block a few times a day; just because the more time you spend with it, the better-equipped you'll be to make moves on the field.

Beyond becoming more comfortable with the ball, there are several other keys to keep in mind that can help turn an average dribbler into an expert one. Most of them have to do with increasing smoothness and fluidity, because that's how the best dribblers operate. In some ways, the ball is just an extension of the player's foot, which means it basically follows along and does whatever the foot does.

Use Both Feet

Most of us are righties. I am, and so when I try to do something new, I almost always try it with my right hand (or foot) first because that's my stronger side. Learning how to dribble (and pass and shoot) is no different.

Thing is, always using your dominant side won't work in soccer. If there's one thing to keep in mind when you—or your child—are learning any soccer skill, it's the importance of using both feet. A player who can dribble or pass or shoot with just one foot is the easiest kind of player to defend. You don't want to be that.

Trying to use your left foot—or right foot, if you're a lefty—will feel incredibly awkward at first. Your foot feels as though it's not even connected to your body. Believe me, that's natural. Do your best to get over that and keep touching the ball with your weaker foot. The more you do it, the sooner you'll feel comfortable dribbling on both sides ... and the sooner you'll be unstoppable on the field.

Heads Up!

You can't beat what you can't see, so keeping your head down as you dribble is a perfect recipe for either getting hurt or giving the ball away.

> **Throw-Ins**
>
> An added benefit of keeping your head up is that you'll also be able to more easily recognize what you hear, as well as what you see. Your teammates or coaches will be calling out "man on!" or "play it back!" and instead of looking up and trying to figure out what they're talking about, you're already there—you see what they see.

It's hard not to look down. I know that. You know that. We all know that. It's only human nature to want to see what's going on with your feet, to make sure the ball is going just where you want it to go.

You've got to trust yourself. If you don't look up, you won't be able to pass the ball to a teammate, which is the way most attacks on goal are set up. You also won't have any idea if you've one opponent or four in your vicinity, or where you are on the field.

I've seen players who are so intent on keeping their heads down that they've literally dribbled the ball out of bounds and didn't know it until they heard the referee's whistle—and not just at the younger age groups! Keeping your head up is something all players struggle with but the best are able to conquer their natural instinct.

Turning

One of the most common dribbling drills (and one you'll see later in this chapter) is the slalom, where players dribble their ball left and right through a series of cones or flags. It's pretty basic, but it's also pretty important because almost no dribbler ever runs in a perfectly straight line.

Being able to turn left and right smoothly is a must. Typically, you want to use the inside of your feet when you cut inside (the inside of your right foot to turn to your left) and the outside of your foot if you're moving outside.

To turn, plant your nondribbling foot hard with the toe pointing in the direction you want to go. Then get your other foot on the opposite side of the ball and either drag it (with the inside of your foot) or push it (with the outside) in the new direction. Remember to use your shielding technique if there's a defender close to you, and don't be afraid to use a full 180-degree turn and look for players who may be behind you.

Fakes and Feints

Good ball control and solid turns will take you far, but you've got to be able to pull off a little wizardry to really dominate as a dribbler. A well-executed fake can open up a passing or shooting lane for you, or just give you more room to keep dribbling.

Here are a few of the more common ball fakes, though you should experiment with what works for you. You may develop one we've never seen before!

- ◆ **Step-over:** Take your right foot and step over the ball without touching it, as though you're going to run left; then push the ball back the other way with the outside of your right foot.

- **Stop-and-go:** Dribble the ball quickly to your left, and then stop suddenly by putting your foot on top of the ball, as if you're changing to the right. After a quick pause, push the ball back to the left with the outside of your left foot.

- *Nutmeg:* With a defender in front of you, push the ball to one side softly, as if you're going to go that way. When the defender starts to follow, tap the ball through his legs and rush past him to pick up the ball on the other side.

- **Behind-the-heel:** As you're dribbling forward, let your left foot get out in front of the ball and then, as you slow down, use your right foot to tap the ball across your body behind your left heel. It'll be hard for the defender to see the ball and you can head in that direction.

def•i•ni•tion

A **nutmeg** is an old soccer term that means to play ball through an opponent's legs. You'll often hear a player who has successfully pulled it off call out "Meg!" as he runs past the hapless defender.

Stop on a Dime

It might sound strange, but stopping is almost as important in dribbling as running. Being able to stop quickly—while maintaining control—is a valuable tool to keeping possession.

If you're running hard in one direction with a defender very close to you, try throwing on the brakes suddenly and watch as he flails to try to stop, too. Those few seconds of breathing room will give you an opportunity to change direction or find the appropriate pass or shot. Remember: just because you're moving doesn't mean you have to keep moving. Sometimes you can go farther by stopping.

Games for U6/U8 Players

As always, the key with younger players is keeping practice games fun. Running through cones with no particular incentive isn't going to keep them interested, so keep the games lightly competitive and get them as many touches on the ball as possible. The more they touch it, the easier it'll become.

Also when dealing with neophyte dribblers, it's best to keep the defensive pressure very low (i.e., don't have other players trying to take the ball from them). As they become more confident, you can increase the amount of defensive presence but do so slowly.

Follow the Leader

This is a great game because it works on touching the ball as well as keeping your head up as you move. In the beginning, it's best for the coach to lead the line, dribbling slowly with his players behind him. When he turns or cuts, they turn or cut. When he does a move, they do a move. Keep it simple and go slow, and make sure there is plenty of space in between each player so no one feels as though he's being trampled.

Red Light/Green Light

It's just as you remember from the playground: each player starts with a ball at his feet on the goal line. A coach stands near midfield. To start the game, the coach calls out "green light!" and turns his back, as the players start dribbling forward; when the coach turns around and calls out "red light!" the players stop right away. If they keep moving or lose control of the ball, they go back to the goal line and start again. This helps teach finding a balance between moving fast and keeping the ball close.

Jailbreak!

Set up a 20×20-yard square (the "jail") with cones or other markers. The players each have a ball and dribble freely in the middle of the square, cutting and moving with the ball at their own pace. When the coach yells out "jailbreak!" the players have to dribble outside the square—not just kicking the ball away and running after it—and the last one out is the jailbird. The players will quickly learn about making cuts and listening to calls from their teammates.

Bulls in the Ring

Everybody takes his ball and spreads out inside a large marked-off area (the penalty area is a good boundary). The coach blows his whistle and each player begins dribbling around at his own pace, trying to keep control of his own ball while also kicking other players' balls out of the area. If a player has his ball kicked away, he comes and sits out. Last player left is the Champion Bull.

Games and Drills for U10/U12 Players

As players get older, their touch on the ball will improve. This is the age when they should start working on harder fakes and cuts, and should practice with a little more defensive pressure to better simulate game action.

Dribbling well and keeping control of the ball after making a move is an exhilarating feeling for a player. The best way to keep kids interested is to have them feel that exhilaration as often as possible, so it becomes natural. That's what these games are designed to do.

Olympic Slalom

Dribbling through cones can be boring, so you want to add a fun element by making it similar to the Olympics. Set up your course (alternating left and right turns), and award "medals" to the top-three finishing times. Make sure players are using their proper foot—left foot when moving left, even if it's harder—to improve feel.

Square Dancing

There's no do-si-do here, but there is a square. Make a square with 20-yard sides, and have players dribble along the edges of it doing a different move on each side. For example, on one side, they'll do step-overs for the whole 20 yards; on another, they'll only use their weaker foot; on a third, they'll only use the outside of their feet; on the last, they'll sprint as fast as they can. Change up what each side calls for and send players after each other no more than 10 seconds apart to encourage quick movement.

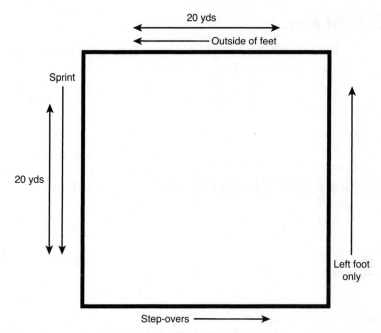

Don't keep the moves assigned to a particular side of the square consistent; change them up routinely, as well as make it mandatory to use your weaker foot on a particular side. The players will become more comfortable using both feet that way.

WELL DONE!

To make this drill a little harder or more advanced, introduce a defender on one or more sides of the square. The dribblers aren't allowed to slow down as they come to that side— they've got to keep moving and make a quick move to try and beat the defender. Whether they do or don't, they retrieve their ball and keep moving.

Juggling

This can be done alone and in groups. It's more fun with at least one other person, because it works both trapping and dribbling. Although there are few instances when juggling is actually used in a game, it's important to do for at least a little while at each practice (or at home) because it increases touch with the ball. If you're juggling with a partner, try to set bars: 5 touches or 10 in a row, or 30 seconds with the ball in the air. It might seem hard at first, but it gets easier the more you do it.

Dribbling Baseball

This is a terrific game and one that kids love because it combines two sports. Set up mini-goals (a few yards wide) in a diamond about 40 feet apart. Designate one player to be the pitcher and put him in the middle. Everyone else is a hitter.

The pitcher passes the ball to the hitter at home plate, who receives it and then tries to dribble the ball toward the first base mini-goal while the pitcher tries to knock the ball away. If the hitter gets to first base, he then tries to go to second as the pitcher tries to stop him there. For each mini-goal the hitter gets through, he gets one point with an extra point if he hits a home run.

This is a game where you want the players to feel comfortable trying out a variety of moves. Encourage them to experiment with different feints and fakes; they might find something that'll work in a game.

If the pitcher is having trouble stopping the hitters, make the mini-goals narrower; if the hitters are having trouble getting past the pitcher, make them wider.

The Least You Need to Know

- Dribbling means using every single part of your foot.
- A one-footed dribbler is an easy mark; learn to use both feet.
- Keep your head up or else you'll watch as someone takes the ball away from you.
- Be creative: try different kinds of fakes to figure out what works for you.
- Stopping at the right time is just as effective a dribbling weapon as running fast.

Chapter **11**

Pass on Grass

In This Chapter

- ◆ Basic passing techniques
- ◆ Using your head
- ◆ Why your voice matters
- ◆ Passing tactics

Even the best dribblers in the world can't spend the whole game running up and down the field with the ball. Passing is the essence of soccer, and a player who knows where and when to make the best pass will always be important to a team.

A big part of passing is common sense: pass the ball to a person who's open! But there are subtleties to soccer passing that separate the good from the great. They're not hard to understand, and after you practice them a little you'll be a passing master.

The Perfect Pass

A pass doesn't have a required distance or speed. It can be 2 feet or 20 yards, it can be in the air or on the ground. That's the beauty of soccer passing—it's up to the player to determine the best way to get the ball from him to his teammate.

We'll get to specific passing fundamentals in a second, but first, here's a short list of things to keep in mind for every pass, regardless of what kind it is:

♦ **Know what you want to do:** Don't just kick the ball to anyone. Make sure each pass has a purpose.

♦ **Keep 'em crisp:** Use soft passes very, very sparingly. Quick passes get to their targets; slow passes get intercepted.

♦ **Open up:** The best pass is typically the one to the player who has the most open space around him. Don't kick the ball to someone just because she's the star. If she's surrounded by defenders, she'll just end up losing the ball.

The Basic, All-Purpose, Use-It-Anywhere Pass

The "vanilla" of soccer passing is a pass that uses the inside of the foot. As you'll see later, the fundamentals of this pass are basically the same as for an outside-of-the-foot pass, but we'll deal first with the inside pass because it's much more common.

So here's the situation: you've trapped the ball perfectly, it's resting at your feet and you look up and spot a teammate ahead of you in a good position. You want to pass him the ball. What do you do? First, you ...

Plant

Let's assume you're going to make this pass with your right foot. That means your left foot is going to be your *plant* foot, or the foot that stabilizes the rest of your body as you deliver the pass. Even though it's not actually touching the ball, the plant foot is critical in any pass.

I was really bad at science in school, so I can't explain the physics behind why it helps to shift your weight on to your left foot as you make a right-footed pass; all I know is that it does.

So as you go to make a pass, you want your plant foot to be a few inches away from the ball with the toe of that foot *pointing in the direction you want the ball to go.* That's important. If you're running forward, and you want the ball to go to the left of you, you've got to adjust your stride so that you can point your plant foot in the direction of the pass. If you don't, the pass won't be very crisp or accurate.

Okay, so back to our situation. You're ready to make the pass and you've got your plant foot all set up. Now, you just …

def•i•ni•tion

The **plant** foot is the nonkicking foot and it provides stability for the player making the pass.

Swing

Coaches will use a million different analogies for how to pass: some say you swing your foot like a hockey stick, some say you should imagine that your foot is a broom. Whatever the image, the point is that you want to raise your right foot, bend your knee slightly, and then swing the foot through so that the side of your foot hits the center of the ball (if you hit too high on the ball, it'll just roll pitifully; too low and it'll pop up).

The inside-of-the-foot pass can be used just about anywhere on the field. It's the first pass a player should learn. Note how the plant foot is a comfortable distance from the ball but right alongside it.

Don't stop when you make contact with the ball, either. Just as in golf or baseball, the follow-through on this swing is very important. In the same way you don't see big-league hitters stop their swings in the middle, you shouldn't drop your foot as soon as it touches the ball. Swing it all the way through, past the point of contact. A good follow-through will make for a crisp pass.

Going Outside

Using the outside of your foot to pass can be a weapon, because defenders aren't often expecting it. The downside, though, is that it's much harder to get good speed on these kinds of passes (again, there's science involved in why—just trust me).

Still, a well-placed outside-of-the-foot pass can be useful, particularly if you're just *flicking* the ball to a teammate nearby.

def•i•ni•tion

Flicking the ball means making a quick pass with either your foot or head, when the ball only barely makes contact with your body as you change its direction.

To do that, you don't have to worry as much about the plant foot; you just flex your ankle to the inside of the ball and then flip it back so the outside of your foot pushes the ball to the side. In other words, you're facing forward but using the outside of your right foot to push the ball to someone who is a few feet away on your right. Simple, yet sneaky!

Hang Time

Getting the ball up in the air is one of those things that seem challenging at first but after you do it a few times becomes easy.

Lifting the ball just requires a few modifications to the basic, all-purpose pass. The plant/swing dynamic is still in effect, but this time you want to plant your foot a little farther from the ball (3 or 4 inches, let's say) and you want to have your weight more on the back of your plant foot instead of the middle.

This "leaning back" feeling is what will lift the ball in the air as you swing your foot through.

Now here's the biggest difference: instead of contacting the ball with the inside of your foot, you're going to use the instep. Remember the instep? It's basically just the front of your foot, where the laces on your cleats are.

WELL DONE!

If your child is having trouble getting the ball up in the air, have her try approaching the ball at a slight angle. Many players find it's easier to hit the ball just below center this way, which is the best way to get it flying quickly.

Point your toe and swing your foot through so your instep goes through the bottom half of the ball, then follow through and watch the ball soar.

The two keys to getting the ball airborne for a lofted pass are plant foot location (a little farther from the ball and a bit behind it) and proper contact with the instep of the foot. Simply put, if you kick the bottom half of the ball, it'll go up.

That's it. That's the standard lofted pass, and the more you lean back, the higher the ball will go. So when do you use this pass? There are

several situations that will often arise during a game which call for
some form of a pass through the air.

Crossing from the Wing

Scoring chances in soccer can develop from anywhere on the field, but
one popular place is from the wings, or sides of the field.

If you watch a high-level game, you'll frequently see a forward dribble
the ball down the sideline, then *cross* the ball into the middle with a
lofted pass. If all goes well, one of his teammates is there to either head
the ball into the goal or trap it, and then pass or shoot.

> **Yellow Card** _____
>
> None of the passes we talk about involve using the toe. Although
> some players, particularly younger ones, might find it easy to get
> the ball in the air by using their toe, it's a bad idea. Toed balls are
> impossible to control, so even if they go in the air, no one will have any
> idea where they're going.

If you're a midfielder or forward, you'll probably be in this situation
at some point, and a well-placed cross can really make it hard for your
opponents to defend. The keys to a good cross are simple:

def•i•ni•tion _____

A **cross** is a pass from the
side of the field into the middle. Some people also call
this kind of pass "centering"
the ball.

- ◆ **Have a strong plant foot:**
  Even if you're sprinting hard
  toward the end line, turn
  your plant foot back toward
  the middle of the field
  before you cross the ball.
  Otherwise, your momentum
  will carry your cross in the
  wrong direction.

- ◆ **Pick out the best target:** In general, aiming for the penalty spot
  is a good target if you're crossing in front of the goal. That's far
  enough away that a goalie can't come grab it, but close enough
  that your teammate should have a very good chance to score.

- ◆ **Vary your height:** Not every cross needs to be a high, soft floater.
  In fact, a lot of times it's good to use a lower, harder cross. Those

are the kinds of balls that defenders don't have time to react to, so your teammates can pounce.

Chipping Over the Top

Another variation on the lofted pass is the *chip*, which is essentially a shorter-distance pass through the air. To do a chip pass, you want to put your plant foot back closer to the ball and really strike down on the bottom half of the ball with your kicking foot. That'll pop the ball up in the air and it'll have backspin on it, so it'll land softly.

When do you use the chip? You'll often see players chipping the ball over top of the last line of defenders so that a teammate can run and catch up to it. That's called chipping "over the top."

def•i•ni•tion

A **chip** is a short pass that pops up in the air.

Get It Out!

The one time when it's okay for a pass not to have a particular destination is when your team is under attack near its own goal, and someone just wants to kick the ball away to safety. An old British coach of mine used to say "anywhere will do" in those situations, meaning that as long as you kicked the ball away, it didn't matter where it went.

In those situations, you want two things: distance and height. The first is obvious: farther from your own goal is better. The second is because no one can steal the ball if it's up in the air. If you kick a hard ball on the ground, it might be intercepted; up in the air, no one can get it.

Throw-Ins

As a goalie, I always appreciated defenders who kept it simple and just kicked the ball out—out of bounds, out of the penalty area, out of danger. Particularly for younger players, the best approach to defending is a simple one: kick it out. No one will ever blame a defender for giving up a throw-in to the other team. It's better than giving up a goal, right?

You can probably guess how this pass goes: strong plant foot, a little farther away from the ball so you've got room to really swing. Use the instep, contact below the equator of the ball, and really follow through—so much so that you'll end with a little hop.

Remember: anywhere will do.

One-Touch Passes

Quick passing is very hard to defend, so a player who can receive a pass and make a pass at the same time is valuable. That's where *one-touch passing* comes in: quite literally, it's moving the ball along to a teammate without ever stopping it.

Think of a one-touch pass as a redirection. Whether you're using the inside, outside, or instep of your foot, you don't have to take nearly as big a swing as you would if the ball were already at your feet. It's already coming toward you with speed, so you just need to decide where you want to send it next, then make contact with your plant foot and body moving in that direction.

def•i•ni•tion

A **one-touch pass** is just what it sounds like—a pass that doesn't involve stopping the ball first. In many ways, it's just a controlled deflection of the ball. You can also take a one-touch shot.

The biggest key to one-touch passing is to keep your eye on the ball. It's a lot easier to mis-kick the ball when it's moving than when it's just sitting at your feet.

Head Games

I suppose you could say that heading the ball is a one-touch pass, but it gets its own section because it's a pretty unique skill. Not hard, of course, but there are a few things to keep in mind when it comes to heading:

◆ **It won't hurt.** Seriously, it won't. At first it might feel a little weird or sting, but if you head the ball the right way, you won't end up with a headache.

WELL DONE!

If you want to help your son work on heading at home, start with a game of catch, soccer-style. Go in the backyard and start just 2 or 3 feet apart. Toss the ball softly to him and he lets it bounce off his forehead right back to you. As he gets more comfortable, you move farther back. Keep track of how many balls in a row he can head back to you, and try to set a new record each night.

◆ So what is the right way? **Ninety-nine percent of the time, you'll want to use your forehead.** Not the top of your head. Not the back. Definitely not the bridge of your nose. Good solid contact on the forehead will give you the best control, best power, and least amount of discomfort.

◆ **Keep your eyes open.** It may be hard at first, but it'll help so much. Keep your eyes open, watch the ball come to your head, and then make contact. Oh, and keep your mouth closed so you don't bite your tongue. Remember: eyes open, mouth closed.

◆ **Neck stiff, back loose.** That means locking your neck before you head the ball, and keeping your back loose so you can arch it and then snap forward to give your header power. The pop doesn't come from waving your neck around; it comes from moving your entire upper body back and through. If you try to use your neck, you'll just end up in pain.

The proper way to head the ball is to keep your eyes open, mouth closed, and watch the ball make contact with your forehead. You provide force to the header by arching and snapping your back—not your neck.

These are the basics of heading the ball as it relates to passing. Heading for goal and heading on defense are covered in those chapters, but these fundamentals apply to them, too.

How to Avoid Passing Headaches

Lots of players don't like heading, so they'll wait for the ball to drop and then control it. You're not one of them. You know that using your head is a big weapon in passing because there are so many different ways you can do it:

- **The set header:** This is basic. The ball is coming toward you in the air. You see a teammate nearby. You set your feet flat, stiffen your neck, and deliver a short snap of your back as the ball hits your forehead, moving it right to your teammate.

- **The side flick:** If you want to pass the ball to the side with your head, the flick is your best tool. You still want to use your forehead, but this time you let the ball deflect off to one side instead of right in the middle. You can loosen your neck just a little and snap it in the direction you want the ball to go.

- **The back flick:** Very similar to the side flick, but this time you relax your neck even more—the only time it's allowed in heading!—and let the ball deflect off your forehead back over you. Basically, you want to lean your head back as the ball approaches and let it glance off you as it goes on its way. This is particularly helpful near the goal as you can flick the ball into a crowded area where teammates can then kick it in.

Get with the Lingo

As important as your feet are to being a good soccer player, your mouth is almost as important. What good is it if you're a great dribbler or shooter but never get the ball because your teammates don't know you're open?

That's why talking is critical. If you've got the ball, you want to listen to hear where your teammates are located; if you want the ball, you've got to call out where you are so someone will pass the ball to you.

Some of the calls are universal and easy to understand. If you're behind a teammate who is approaching a defender, for example, you could call "support back!" to let him know he can turn and give you the ball.

If you're parallel with a teammate, you can call out "square right!" or "square left!" depending on which side you're on. Why square? It doesn't make total sense (because there's no actual square involved), but it's because the angle of the pass is a straight angle, as though the ball is moving along one side of a square.

Other calls may vary from team to team, but the important thing to remember is to talk—a lot. The more information you give (or get), the easier it will be to make the right passes.

Passing Tactics

Not all passes are isolated events. Remember earlier when we said every pass should have a purpose? Some passes are designed to simply move the ball from one player to another, but others have more behind them. They're specifically designed to set up a scoring chance, say, or free up a teammate who is moving toward open space.

There are so many different possible passing sequences, but there are a few common passing tactics that crop up all the time in soccer games.

The Lead

Some passes go right to a player's feet, but sometimes you're passing to a moving target. In those cases, you want to *lead* your teammate, which basically means you want to pass the ball to where he's going, not where he's been.

In other words, if you want to pass to someone running down the wing, kick the ball out in front of him, so it rolls into his path. In soccer, this is called *running on to the ball.*

def•i•ni•tion

A **lead** pass is one played ahead of its intended target so that the player can **run on to the ball,** or receive it in stride.

How hard or soft should you kick it? There's no magic formula, and after you've got some experience with how fast your teammates run, it'll be easier. A good rule of thumb, though, is that it's usually better to overestimate how much to lead someone. It's harder for a teammate to double back than it is to run a little farther.

Give-and-Go

This passing play is just the same as it is in basketball. You pass the ball to a teammate, then get it right back from them, typically after you've run a few feet in one direction.

Because it's pretty cumbersome to yell out "give-and-go!" you'll often hear players call "one-two" when they want a give-and-go, referring to the two-step process of the play. This kind of pass is also occasionally called a "wall pass."

Through Balls

A through ball is a pass that, literally, goes through the defense and into space behind defenders so that an attacker can run on to it. If you hear an attacker call "through!" it means to send a ball behind the defense, because the attacker believes he'll be able to get to the ball first.

Games for U6/U8 Players

There are a ton of great passing games that will keep younger soccer players interested in what they're doing, while at the same time honing their skills. At the youngest ages, you just want players to begin to feel comfortable with the idea that they are able to move the ball quickly and accurately from one teammate to another.

Duckpin Bowling

This is a good basic game either for groups or at home. Set up 10 cones at varying distances from you—three within 5 to 10 feet, three around 15 to 20 feet, and four even farther, for example. Then start trying to knock down one pin after another with the all-purpose inside-of-the-foot pass, starting with the shorter distances and moving to the longer ones.

If you're playing against someone, alternate shots. If it's a larger group, set up several "alleys" and make it a relay race; two people to an alley, one "bowler," and one player who stands among the pins and rolls the ball back after each shot. First lane to knock down all 10 cones wins.

Mini-Golf

You'll need some room for this one, but if you've got a big field or open space, it's a lot of fun. Using cones, set up a "course" of golf holes which require different kinds of passes. A lofted pass for the "tee shot" followed by a chip to get on the green and an inside-of-the-foot pass for the putt. You can draw boundaries (with cones, string, or tape) and even build in distractions (have to pass through a coach's legs, for example). Have fun with the course setup and, if it gets too easy, have the kids try playing a hole with their weaker foot.

Monkey in the Middle

This game requires three players and a ball. Two players keep passing the ball back and forth, while the third player—the monkey—has to try and steal it. If he does, he gets to go to the outside and the player who last touched the ball becomes the monkey. As players get better at passing, decrease the space of the field they're playing in to encourage crisper passing.

Spud!

Remember this game from recess? Give each player a different number. Then gather all the players around in a circle, and toss the ball up in the air. As soon as the ball is in the air, the players can run in any direction except for the player who was assigned the number called; he's got to step in and trap the ball. Then he gets to take four steps—S, P, U, D—in any direction, before trying to hit one of the other players with an on the ground, all-purpose pass.

If he misses, he gets a letter (an "S" for the first, "P" for the second, etc.). If he hits, the player he hits gets a letter. Anyone who gets all four letters is out!

Games and Drills for U10/U12

Passing fundamentals are the same, regardless of age, but as players get older it's the nuances that become more important. A crisp, accurate pass becomes the norm, as opposed to the rarity, and players need to be more confident with their communication, as well as their decision-making. These games and drills should help with both.

Guard the Castle

Set up a 12×12-yard grid with cones, and put one more cone in the middle (if you have discs, put a ball on top of the disc in the middle). The object of the game is for three players moving on the perimeter of the grid to pass the ball around to each other while a defender—who must stay inside the grid—tries to steal it.

The players on the outside score points if they are able to successfully knock the cone in the middle over; the defender is only able to become one of the perimeter players by stealing the ball. The players on the outside will need to move the ball quickly to get a clear shot at the cone in the middle, and communication is key.

5 vs. 2 in the Box

Keep that 12×12-yard grid, but this time put five players anywhere in the box, with the rest of the players lined up in groups of two outside one of the corners. The first group of two passes the ball into the grid, then steps in and begins trying to steal the ball from the five attackers, who must keep the ball moving. If the defenders can't get the ball in 30 seconds, their turn is over and the next pair gets a chance. If they do steal it, they become attackers and two attackers join the defenders' line.

This drill reinforces the skills needed to pass in a confined space—something that often happens in the midfield of a tight game.

Combinations

This drill sounds more complex than it actually is, but it's great at improving a player's ability to work with give-and-go passes.

Start with a grid that's approximately 20×25 yards in a rectangle. Put one player at three corners with the rest of the players in a line at the fourth. This is where the drill starts.

The first player in line at corner A (see figure) passes to the player at corner B, then follows his pass. Player B one-touches the ball back into Player A's path, then runs around his corner cone and heads toward Player C. Player A passes the ball to Player C, who one-touches it into Player B's path, then runs around his cone and heads toward Player D. Player B passes to Player D, who one-touches it into Player C's path and so on.

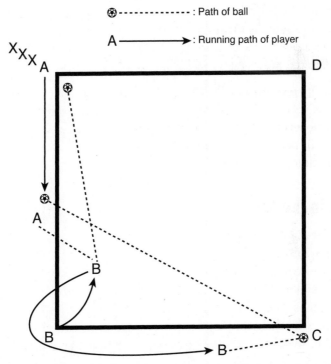

The important part of this drill is to keep the ball moving. If it's done right, every touch will be a pass with no stopping. By the end of it, everyone will be more comfortable with the idea of passing and moving.

Mini-Goals

Being able to pass accurately on the run is a valuable skill, and this drill puts that at a premium. Set up two "goals" which are only 1 yard wide and about 40 yards from each other. Put one player next to each of them (the "servers"), with two other players halfway between them.

The drill begins with one player sprinting toward one goal while the other sprints to the opposite one. The servers pass the ball out to the players, who must quickly trap and then try to pass the ball into the "goals." They then turn and sprint in the opposite direction to do the same thing at the other goal. Each group of two players does this for 60 to 90 seconds, keeping track of how many "goals" they score.

It's important in this drill for the players to keep moving, and for the servers to be accurate with their passes.

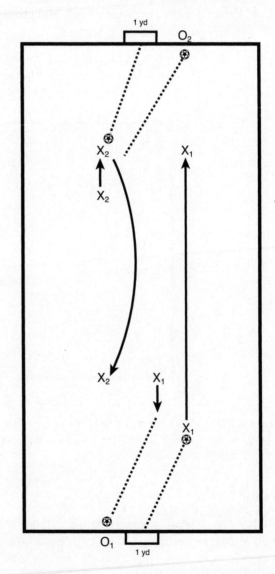

The Least You Need to Know

♦ There are a variety of ways to pass the ball, but it's important to have your plant foot in the right spot for almost all of them. If the plant is off, the pass probably will be, too.

♦ Choosing the right target is as important as the pass itself. Give the ball to a player who can do something with it, not just the player who is closest or most-skilled.

♦ Passes can go in any direction. Sometimes the best way to get forward is to pass back.

♦ Talk and listen. Communication between teammates is the only way to know which pass will best help the team.

Chapter 12

Nothing but Nets

In This Chapter

- ◆ The fundamentals of shooting
- ◆ More advanced techniques for scoring
- ◆ Making it hard for the goalie
- ◆ Dealing with penalty kicks

You can't win if you don't score and you can't score if you don't shoot. Do you need any other reasons to make clear how important shooting is?

Scoring a goal is the most exhilarating part of playing soccer, and it's also highly addictive: the more you do it, the more you want to do it again. Don't worry though; after you've got these shooting basics down, that shouldn't be a problem.

Strike It Flush

Want to know the secret to being a good shooter? It's pretty simple: making good contact. The most powerful, most accurate shots are the ones that come from clean strikes of the ball.

Sometimes you'll use the inside of your foot to shoot—basically a harder version of the all-purpose pass—but the majority of shots are taken with the instep of a player's foot, so that's what we're going to focus on in this chapter (except for one part about heading for goal).

Laces Up

Most beginning soccer players assume that their toes are the best part of the foot to use for shooting. In reality, toed shots are the worst ones because they're impossible to keep under control.

Instead, the instep—also known as the part of your foot where the laces on your cleats are located—is the primary shooting surface. As you approach the ball, you want to point your toe down so that the instep can hit the ball flush (not at an angle), giving you maximum power and accuracy.

Self-Support

Remember how important the plant leg was to passing? It's even more critical in shooting. Let's assume you're shooting with your right foot. As you approach the ball, you want your left foot to be alongside the ball, about 6 inches away from it and with the toe pointed where you want the shot to go.

For the basic shot, you want your plant foot alongside the ball and the knee on your shooting leg over the ball. This will help keep the shot down and give you the most power.

Unlike with the lofted pass, you don't want the plant foot to be behind the ball much at all; if it is, you'll see a lot of shots flying over the goal instead of into it.

Get On Top

To really get a bullet shot, you want your weight to be over the ball when you strike it. An old coach of mine used to tell us that you almost want to feel as though you're falling forward when you shoot, because if you lean back it saps the power you're getting and will just lift the ball in the air.

Another way to think of it is to picture your right knee being directly above the ball as your right foot makes contact with it. If it is, you know your weight is properly positioned. If it's not, you're probably off balance.

The motion of the shot comes from your entire body, not just your leg. After your plant foot is set, swing your shooting foot through with your toe pointed down and the laces square, striking the middle of the ball. The ball should fly on a low line, with good speed, in the direction your plant foot is pointing.

Perfect Landing

Can you imagine what a golf swing would be like if you tried to stop it right at impact? Not good, right?

Follow-through is just as important in soccer. A well-struck shot requires a strong follow-through, and the best way to know if you're doing it right is to look at which foot you land on after the shot. If it's the same one you took the shot with, you're golden; if it's the plant foot, you're not even coming close to the kind of power you ought to be getting.

Think of it this way: when you take a shot, your weight is supposed to be forward. You're also supposed to swing your leg through way beyond the ball, just as you'd do with a golf club.

> **Throw-Ins** _____
>
> I remember a game when I was younger in which my team was losing by a goal and there was a big scramble in front of the other team's goal. Suddenly, the ball was rolling toward one of my teammates who was standing inside the goal area—less than 6 yards from the net!—and he leaned back as he shot the ball. It soared over the top, the other team got a goal kick, and we lost by one.
>
> Moral of the story? You're never so close to the goal that you can't get the ball over the bar. Keep your weight forward on every shot. Your teammates will thank you.

So if you do both of those things, there will be a natural "hop" that will occur and that should make you land on your right foot (if you've taken a right-footed shot). This is particularly important if the ball is rolling toward you. Stay forward and the ball will stay down. Then all you've got to do is look up and see the goalie taking the ball out of the back of the net.

Making a Mark

Have you ever seen someone shoot a hole in someone with a soccer ball? Me neither. That's why a well-placed shot is always preferred to an incredibly powerful one.

Where are the best places to shoot? The snarky answer is "where the goalie can't get to" but there are some general tenets to keep in mind when it comes to shooting:

- ◆ **Low is better than high.** Goalies have better reach with their hands than their feet, so high shots are more easily swatted away.

- ◆ **Go for the fat part of the net.** If you're approaching the goal on an angle, shoot to the far side instead of the near side. Why? There's more room there.

- ◆ **Follow your shot.** Wherever you shoot, don't just stand there and watch what happens. Land on your shooting foot and keep running toward the goal in case there's a rebound. That way if you don't score with your first shot, you might with your second.

Yellow Card _____

Players at the youngest ages may quickly find that shooting high is a good way to score because the goalies—and everyone else—aren't very tall. Although this might work for a few years, it's a bad habit to develop; as everyone gets older (and taller), high shots won't be nearly as effective. The sooner a player learns to shoot low, the better off he'll be.

These are just a few things to keep in mind when you're preparing to shoot. Above all else, you need to trust yourself. Glance up, pick an area to shoot at, and then look back at the ball while you swing your leg through.

Trusting your own ability might be the hardest part of successful shooting. The more you shoot, the more confident you'll feel that the ball will go where you want. That sort of feeling is one of those things that is learned, but can't really be taught.

The Shot That Can't Be Stopped

As a goalie, I quickly learned that the hardest shots to stop are the ones that are low to the ground, moving with decent speed, and headed toward the back posts of the goal (sometimes called the *struts*).

Even if a goalie is good at diving, it's almost impossible to get all the way down to the ground and all the way over to the post in time to knock away a shot with good speed. As cool as it might be to shoot for the upper corners, those are the ones that I could leap for and deflect or, more likely, watch sail over the crossbar.

If you're serious about scoring, work on shooting the ball so it bounces off the strut at the back of each corner. If you can do that regularly, you'll be celebrating plenty of goals on the field during games. Even the best goalies won't be able to stop shots such as these.

Advanced Shooting

The basic shot isn't too tough to master, but the reality is that not all shots in games will be so straightforward. There will be times when you'll have to improvise a little to get a shot on goal, and these are the situations that can turn out to be pretty memorable.

def•i•ni•tion

A **finisher** is another name for an attacker who is particularly good at converting scoring chances.

Is it worth practicing these techniques? It is, especially if you've become pretty proficient at hitting targets with the basic shot. If you've got that down, these skills might be what sets you apart as a real *finisher* instead of just another forward.

Around the Bend

Although it might be good to be a straight shooter in life, it's not always the best thing in soccer. Sometimes, you're going to want to curve the ball, particularly if it'll help you get a shot around a wall of defenders and into the goal.

So how do you *bend* or swerve the ball to your advantage? Imagine a clock face. Normally, you'd strike the ball right in the middle (between the 12 and 6) for a shot. To bend the ball from right to left, however, you've got to hit it closer to 3 o'clock; to make it go left to right, you hit it closer to 9 o'clock.

def•i•ni•tion

If you want to shoot the ball that curves, you'll have to **bend** the ball by using a different technique. Sometimes you'll also hear players saying they "swerved" the ball, which means the same thing.

The key to both is to make a glancing blow. If you're shooting with your right foot and bending the ball from left to right, you'll almost feel the ball rolling off your instep and on to the inside of your foot; for swerves from left to right, you should feel it rolling from the instep to the outside of the foot.

Trust me, it takes practice. Take a few balls out and just start kicking. After a few shots, I promise your shots will be curving.

Volleys and Half-Volleys

Opportunistic scorers know that some scoring chances come when the ball is already in the air: a cross from the wing, a deflection off a defender, or a chip over the top. In these situations, there may not be time to trap the ball and then shoot it. That's where volleys and half-volleys come in.

A *volley* is a one-touch shot and the basics are the same as they are for a regular shot: keep your eyes on the ball, your toes pointed down, and follow through. Landing on your shooting leg is even more important because the already elevated ball will soar high (and over the goal) if you lean back.

A *half-volley* is a volley struck when the ball has just bounced off the ground. In other words, instead of shooting the ball out of mid-air, you let the ball bounce and then kick it a split-second later, as it's rising. These shots take precise timing and can be tricky; stubbed toes are a common side affect of half-volley practice. Still, they're a worthwhile weapon because they can often catch a goalkeeper by surprise.

def•i•ni•tion

A **volley** is a shot played directly out of the air. A **half-volley** is one that's played a split-second after the ball bounces off the ground.

Getting Ahead

A powerful, well-struck header from close range is one of the toughest shots for a goalie to stop and the truth is that they're not so tough to pull off. We already went over the basics of heading, and there are only a few modifications to make when it comes to heading for goal.

The first is the target. Although you might think you should just head the ball on a line into the net, the best way to score is to head the ball down. Remember what we said about the hardest shots to stop? Heading the ball on a line means it'll be around shoulder height—easy pickings for the goalie. Head it down and it'll bank off the back strut of the goal, just like you want.

WELL DONE!

Kids may see older players executing diving headers during games and want to mimic them. It's tough to discourage, so if you want to help them practice this tough skill at home, try this: have them kneel on all fours in the backyard grass, and toss a ball up in the air in front of them. They should then shoot forward and head the ball, landing softly on their stomachs. This way, they get to practice the "diving header" but are already low to the ground, decreasing the chance they'll get hurt.

The next key is getting power. This comes from a strong arch and snap in your back, not by flopping your neck. If a cross is floating in the goal area, by all means jump up and try to head it. But whether you jump or not, bend your back and then snap forward so your forehead hits the ball. It'll have plenty of force and you can keep your neck stiff the entire time.

Lastly, focus on placement. Just as a regular shot, it matters less how hard you head the ball and more where you head it. Pick out a corner and try to put the ball there instead of worrying about how much snap you're getting. Keep your eyes on the ball as it hits your forehead, and then watch the net ripple.

Scissors and Bicycle Kicks

I put this section in because you may see more advanced players trying these maneuvers, but they're not for beginners (unless you think injuries are fun). A *scissors kick* is a volley done while the player has turned sideways, his legs moving like a scissors to shoot the ball out of the air. It's a move that requires very precise timing and a lot of agility. Basically, the player jumps up and turns sideways while moving his legs to volley the ball, then lands on the ground.

A *bicycle kick*, or overhead kick, is used when a player has her back to the goal and literally falls backward while kicking the ball. It's very, very

def•i•ni•tion

A **scissors kick** is done with the player jumping so that their body is sideways, and then kicking their legs in a scissor motion. A **bicycle kick** is an exciting (and dangerous) play where a player falls backward and kicks the ball over his head.

easy to hurt yourself doing this kick and although pros may make it look easy, many referees in youth games will whistle it as "dangerous play." Proceed with caution.

About Those Penalty Kicks

Taking penalty kicks is an honor that most coaches usually give to their best shooters. Scoring from only 12 yards away seems easy, but it takes a strong nerve to convert consistently. How can you become a go-to penalty taker?

◆ **Pick a side:** As soon as you find out you will be taking the kick, pick which corner of the goal you're going to shoot at.

◆ **Head down:** After you've chosen, take a short run-up and keep your head down as you shoot to that corner, aiming to hit the strut in the back corner of the goal. Don't be afraid to use the inside of your foot, instead of your instep, if you're more comfortable with that. Just keep your head down and make solid contact. This way you won't see the goalie moving around trying to distract you.

◆ **Don't be psyched out:** Goalies will try anything to rattle shooters. Don't sweat any of it. Even if the goalie does happen to dive to the same side you pick, a strong shot to the strut will be impossible for him to stop anyway.

Nobody scores every single time he takes a penalty kick, but if you're confident in your approach, you'll make a whole lot more than you miss.

Games for U6/U8 Players

In the beginning, you just want young players to get comfortable with the idea of picking a target and hitting it. When that concept has settled in, working on accuracy and precision with shooting follows naturally. Shooting games are fun for all players, young or old, so there's really no way to go wrong in choosing a way to practice scoring.

Hit the Coach

Fun for everyone except the adult in the middle. Have the players form a circle around you, say, 10 yards away, each with a ball. On your signal, everyone tries to hit you with a shot. Kids love this game and it's a great way to get them laughing, while also focusing on how to get the ball to go where they want. As your welts grow, move the players back. After awhile, you'll see them hitting the back struts just the way they were hitting you.

Arcade Shooting

Set up a 15×15-yard grid, with five disc-cones scattered randomly within it. Put another disc-cone upside down on top of each one.

Players are in groups of two, with one player shooting and the other player retrieving the off-target shots. Each group tries to knock over all five disc-cones in the shortest amount of time possible. This game stresses the importance of shooting accuracy over power.

Birthday Piñata

Remember how much fun it was to bash the piñata and get the candy? Same approach here. Fill up two shopping bags with candy (or pieces of gum, if you don't want to do sweets), and tape them shut. Then tie them to each post on the goal, and have the players take turns trying to bust the bag with a shot from 15 to 20 yards away. It's a perfect end-of-practice drill and the one who breaks the bag will be a hero!

Wall Ball

If you've got access to a practice wall (either on grass or blacktop), this is a great game for getting players comfortable with volleys and one-touch shooting.

First, chalk a "goal" on the wall that's about 5 yards wide and 6 feet high. The players then line up and the first one shoots the ball into the goal on the wall. The next player has to volley the rebound into the goal, with the player behind him doing the same, and so on. If a player misses, he gets an out. Three outs and you step out of line.

Games and Drills for U10/U12 Players

As players get more experience, shooting practice can become more pressurized in an effort to simulate game-conditions. Remember: accuracy is more important than power. There's no extra credit for how fast the ball is moving when it goes in the goal.

Cat-and-Mouse

This is a drill teams often use to warm up before games because it gets the shooting muscles loose. Have a line of players about 35 yards from the goal and another line of players at the top of the penalty area. The first player in line one passes the ball to the first player in line two. The player at the penalty area gives a one-touch pass back into the original player's path, then offers very passive defensive pressure as he takes one or two touches and shoots on goal.

The second player shouldn't try to steal the ball. She just wants to make the first player take a dribble or two and then shoot on the run.

Soccer Tennis

Each side of the "court" should be a 12-yard square, though you can adjust this if there are more or less people (three on a side is the norm). Each point starts with one side "serving" the ball to the other by volleying the ball over the center line on the fly.

The receiving team can let the ball bounce one time, and can pass it amongst themselves (with no more than one bounce) up to three times before volleying it back. If the ball goes out or bounces more than once, the other team gets a point. Play to 7 or 11.

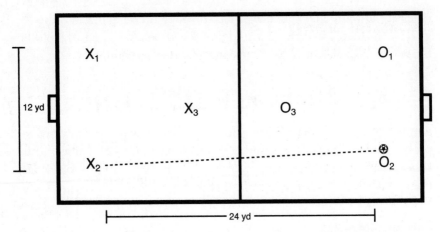

This game is a great warm-up drill early in practice and gets players comfortable with one-touch shooting. Go from this to a game that involves volleying on net and watch how much more consistent the shooting is.

Wall Pass Drill

Player A is the attacker and he starts just outside the penalty area, facing Player B, the defender. Players 1 and 2 are stationed on either side of the penalty spot, about 8 yards apart.

The object of the game is for Player A to hit one of the struts at the back of the goal. He does so by dribbling around Player B and/or passing the ball to Players 1 and 2, who can only give wall passes back.

If shooting for the back struts is too challenging, use a modified goal that's 5 yards wide.

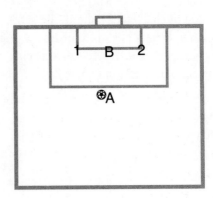

The Shooting Gallery

This is an obstacle course of goal scoring and is a great fitness test, too. Have each player start just outside the penalty area with a ball. First, they must take a basic shot into one of the corners of the goal. Then they run to the penalty spot, where they must take a one-touch shot of a ball passed to them. Next they run to one side of the goal box and head a ball tossed to them into the net, then quickly to the other side for the same thing. Finish the drill by running back toward the penalty spot, receiving one last pass, and then spinning and shooting.

The Least You Need to Know

◆ Keep your weight forward to keep your shots down. If you lean back as you shoot, the ball will usually end up flying over the crossbar.

◆ Accuracy is more important than power. Pick a spot and put the ball there; don't just shoot as hard as you can and expect to score very often.

◆ The hardest shots to stop are the ones that are low and to the corners. Soaring shots may look pretty, but they're much easier for goalies to save.

◆ Confidence comes with repetition. Trust yourself to keep your head down when you shoot. If you do, you'll look up to see the ball in the net more often.

Chapter 13

Keeper of the Flame

In This Chapter

- ◆ Proper positioning
- ◆ How to have sticky fingers
- ◆ Diving like a pro
- ◆ Getting the ball to your teammates

The goalie is the most important player on the field, and I'm not just saying that because I used to be one. As the last line of defense, any big mistake the goalie makes results in the other team scoring. How many other players on the field can say that?

To paraphrase Yoda from *Star Wars*, with great pressure comes great responsibility and that's what playing goalie is all about. It's actually kind of a double-edged sword: everyone is looking at you, which makes it tough. But everyone is looking at you, which makes it kind of exciting, too!

The Great Wall

Goalies are different. It's a fact of soccer life. They can use their hands, they wear funny-colored shirts, and they don't spend most the game running around. Their job is simple: keep the ball out of the net.

Yellow Card

I knew I wanted to be a goalie early on, but I still spent some time playing in the field until I was closer to middle-school or high-school age.

Don't be too quick to pigeonhole a goalie. It's probably a good idea to play both in goal and on the field for a while, at least until the games become more competitive. A well-rounded player is always a valuable one.

So how do they do it? As you'll see in this chapter, a lot of the work comes before an opponent even shoots the ball. Proper positioning is important, as is the right attitude. The best goalies look at the ball as a possession. It belongs to them. And anytime it comes near them, they are going to go out and take it, no matter what they have to do.

The Angle

You'll often hear coaches talking about "narrowing the angle" or "cutting the angle," but what does that mean? For a goalie, it means putting yourself in a place where the goal looks smallest to the attacker.

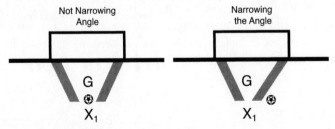

The closer you are to the ball, the less room the shooter can see on either side of you. Just be careful you don't get too close; a tricky shooter will chip the ball over you!

Think of it this way: if you're standing on the goal line and the shooter is at the top of the penalty area, the goal will look very wide to him. If you're standing at the top of the goal area, on the other hand, the goal looks smaller to the attacker because you're closer to him. You've "narrowed the angle" of his shot.

This is a long way of saying that you shouldn't just stay in the middle of the goal and you shouldn't just stay on the goal line. Always be thinking about where the shooter is and how you can step up to narrow his angle on goal.

The Stance

The basic stance for a goalie is an athletic one. Knees bent, feet and ankles loose, hands out at your sides with palms open and facing forward.

One of my first goalkeeping coaches taught me a small detail that many goalies miss: keep your hands low, not high. A lot of goalies have their default position with their hands above their hips, their fingers facing up instead of down.

The proper way is the reverse. Why? Because it's easier to shoot your hands up quickly then it is to bring them down, plus the hardest shots to stop are the low ones. You might as well be in the best position possible to try and handle them.

The Split-Step

After you're in your basic stance, you want to keep moving. The worst thing a goalie can do is be flat-footed, because it's so much harder to make a save from a dead stop.

In anticipation of a shot, most goalies will do something called a *split-step*. Athletes in many other sports use this move, too, including fielders in baseball and tennis players.

Basically, it's just a tiny step forward with one foot followed by a

def•i•ni•tion

A **split-step** is a move in which you step forward with one foot then bring the second foot up parallel in an athletic stance. The weight should be on the balls of your feet the entire time.

spreading of the two feet into an athletic stance, with the weight on the balls of your feet. This puts your body in motion and makes it easy to shift left or right, up or down depending on where the shot is going.

The "W"

Catching shots is always the preferred save for a goalie because that way there is no rebound for the other team to pounce on. The safest way to consistently hold on to shots—regardless of how hard they're coming—is to position your hands in "the W."

Put both hands out in front of you with your fingers spread and the tips of your two thumbs touching. Your hands look like a W, right?

That's basically how your hands should be when it comes time to catch a shot, too. Obviously your thumbs don't need to be jammed up against each other, but they should be close. That way, there's no chance the ball will sneak through your fingers and get past you (or, just as painful but in a different way, smack you in the nose!).

If you use "the W," there's almost no chance the ball will be able to slip through your fingers.

WELL DONE!

The most important aspect of stopping any shot is to get as much of your body behind the ball as possible. If it's a slow roller, drop down to one knee and pick it up; if it's a shot at your midsection, cradle it into your stomach. The more of your body you have behind the ball, the less chance there is it'll get past you.

Palming/Tipping

Sometimes a shot can't be caught because it's too far away or too high to get both hands to safely. In these instances a goalie wants to palm or tip the ball away from the goal—oftentimes out of bounds—instead of risking a difficult catch that ends up being dropped right in front of the goal.

To palm a ball away from the goal, remember to use as much of your hand as you can get on the ball. If you can, push the ball to the side, perhaps even past the post so it goes out of bounds for a corner kick. That way there won't be a quick rebound you can't handle.

On high shots that are coming in fast, it may be best to tip the ball over the crossbar. To do this move you just need to angle your hand slightly (pointing the palm up a bit) and the ball should hit it and ricochet high over the bar.

Coaches rightfully say all the time that it's always better to palm or tip the ball out of bounds than it is to try and catch a shot that's too difficult. Remember: better to give up a corner kick than give up a goal.

The High Ball

Being a goalie means more than just dealing with shots. A goalie also has to take control of the area near the goal by dealing with crosses and passes that are floating in the air.

Obviously the first choice is to simply come and catch these balls, keeping the opponents from heading the ball on goal. But there are also times when a big crowd of people may make it hard to catch a cross.

The best alternative in these situations is to punch the ball away. This move, also called "boxing" the ball, is done with one or two fists but the key in either case is to make contact with the flat surface of your knuckles and get the ball as high and as far as possible. The best punches soar out the sides of the penalty area—away from danger and, hopefully, into the path of a teammate who can start an attack.

Get on the Ground!

Making an acrobatic diving save is what every goalie lives for because, really, it's the goalie's version of a highlight-reel goal. A great save is something people remember and it can also change the feel of an entire game.

Diving saves aren't hard to do, but there are a few steps a goalie should take to increase their effectiveness and decrease the chance of getting hurt.

Power Step to Success

With the goal being 8 yards wide, most of the time a goalie's dive is toward one of the posts in an attempt to keep out a shot that's headed for the corner. These are situations where you need to cover some ground quickly.

The key is something called a *power step*, which is basically exactly what it sounds like. If you're diving to your right, instead of turning your body and using two feet to dive in that direction (as you might off the edge of a pool), stay facing the field and just turn your foot so your right toes are pointed at that post and step hard in that direction. That's your power step.

Throw-Ins

High-flying dives are definitely an advanced move, but the process is basically the same: everything starts with a power step, only this time you use your other leg to catapult yourself into the air. I went to a goalie camp once where one of the counselors was a national team goalie who could literally get his body parallel to the crossbar with his dives. It was absolutely amazing and it all started with a power step.

With that foot now established as your base, shoot your left leg across your body in the same direction as you push off your right. This will give you the force you need to dive toward the post, while keeping your body facing the field so you can see the shot and reach your hand out as far as possible to try and stop it.

The Raspberry-Free Dive

Lots of goalies wear special shorts that have padding in the hips and many also wear spandex underneath to help avoid those nasty welts and raspberries that can crop up from lots of diving and sliding.

There's no surefire way to avoid all that redness, but using the proper form on low dives will make the whole thing less painful. My coach used to tell me to try to visualize getting my body to the ground as quickly possible. That is, instead of diving through the air and falling to the ground near the post where the shot is headed, I should try to get my arms out and almost hydroplane over there.

What's the difference? Well, first, by sliding there's no chance you'll crack a bone in your hip or elbow by landing awkwardly, and second, there's no chance you'll over-estimate your dive and fly over the ball as it rolls into the net underneath you.

The Secret to Stopping More Shots

Let's say your diving form is top-notch now. You've got the power step down, you're sliding along the grass instead of flying through the air whenever possible, and your hands are always starting low instead of high. That's it, right?

Not exactly. One tip many goalies forget about is the *direction* of their dives. I know, it sounds dumb. *Direction? I dive toward the ball, duh!* But there's more to it than that.

If a shot is headed toward the right post and you're stationed a few yards off the goal line, the natural inclination is to dive backward toward the post. That's where the ball is going, so why shouldn't you go there, too?

Truth is, diving with a slightly forward angle is a much better idea. Not only will you be able to cover more ground with your dive, but there's a much lower chance you'll deflect the ball into the goal if you're going forward instead of backward.

Remember, with your split-step you're already moving forward anyway. Keep going in that direction. If you go back, you'll only be hurting yourself.

Yes, General Goalie, Sir!

Many people compare playing goalie to being a quarterback and, in at least one way, it's a good analogy. Both positions require the players playing them to be a vocal leader.

> **Throw-Ins**
>
> Don't worry too much about offending your teammates by barking directions at them. Former Manchester United goalie Peter Schmeichel was notorious for his screams of rage at his defenders. Sometimes it looked as though he was angrier at them than he was at the other team (and maybe he was!), but he usually ended up getting his way—and United usually ended up winning.

As the goalie, you've got to be the one taking charge. If you call for the ball, the other players are supposed to get out of the way and let you take it, no questions asked. When it comes to anything in your half of the field, you should be yelling, screaming, waving, and doing whatever else it takes to get your teammates to understand what they need to do to help protect the goal.

Needless to say, it's pretty rare to find a shy goalkeeper.

Organizing the Defense

This is an ongoing job for the goalie, so basically you'll be constantly asking yourself two questions: Are all the attackers being covered right now? And who should be on whom?

If you see one of the opposing forwards moving freely, you should quickly be calling out his number and location and demanding that one of your teammates get on him right away. Don't be bashful: *Jimmy! Pick up number 14 at the back post!* and then make sure Jimmy gets there.

Setting the Wall

If the opponents are awarded a free kick near your goal area, the first thing you'll want to do is set up the *wall*. This is basically a row of your teammates who stand next to each other 10 yards away from the kick in an effort to block an area of the goal from the shooter. The idea is that the goalie will have the wall set up to obstruct one half of the goal while she takes care of the other half.

To set up the wall, first call out the number of players you want in it (*Three! Three in the wall! Three!*) and then move next to the goalpost on the side you want the wall to cover. With your face up against the post, motion with your hand left and right until the outside player in the wall appears to be covering the post. The rest of the players then go next to that player, and you move to the other side of the goal so you can see the shot. If the shooter shoots right, he'll drive it into the wall; if he shoots left, you'll be able to save it.

Saving Penalty Kicks

No goalie likes penalty kicks because … well, because what's to like about someone getting a free shot at goal from 12 yards away with no one but you standing in the way?

Although a perfectly placed penalty kick is pretty much impossible to stop, the reality is that most penalties aren't perfect, so there are a few things you can do to give yourself the best chance of pulling off a "miracle" save:

- ◆ **Make yourself big:** Keep your arms out wide and stand tall. The bigger you look, the smaller the goal looks, and the tighter the shooter may get as he prepares to kick.

- ◆ **Be distracting:** The rules say you're not allowed to move forward from the goal line until the kick is taken, but there's no law against moving side-to-side. As the kicker is getting read to shoot, shimmy sideways a little with your arms up and down. It'll make it harder for the shooter to focus.

◆ **Make a decision:** Some goalies like to try and guess which side of the goal the shooter will go for, then dive that way just before he shoots in hopes they're right. Others like to stay in the middle and react, hoping the shot is close enough to them that they can save it. There's no fool-proof method; just pick the one you like most and go with it.

There's also no substitute for knowledge. If you're watching a game and there's a penalty kick, see which side the shooter aims at. You never know when you might face the same team and same shooter; if you do, there's a good chance he'll end up shooting the same way.

> **WELL DONE!**
>
> One trick that used to help me save penalties was to watch the shooter's eyes. Not just as he's taking the shot, but even before. Watch him as he's getting ready to kick and see if he looks over at one corner of the goal. There's a good chance he's checking out the area at which he's planning to shoot.

Giving Handouts

Getting possession of the ball is only part of the job for a goalie. He's also got to be able to get the ball to his teammates and start an attack. This is often called distribution, and there are a few common ways to do it:

◆ **Rolling:** This is just like bowling the ball. Get low to the ground so the ball doesn't bounce or skip, and just roll it out there with one hand.

◆ **Throwing:** You can either wing the ball side-arm or, for better distance and accuracy, throw it over-arm. Cup the ball in your hand and wrist, and then swing your arm over the top hard. The ball should fly straight.

◆ **Punting:** A *punt* is when you drop the ball from your hand and boot it before it hits the ground, just as in football. In soccer, though, you can drop the ball with one or two hands. Try it different ways and see what's comfortable.

The key with all methods of distribution is to get the ball to a team-mate. Obviously a punt is a little different (you're mostly just aiming for an area of the field), but the hope is that—just as a regular player—each pass has a purpose.

Games and Drills for Keepers

There are a number of ways to practice goalie skills and most of them are universal to all keepers—young and old. Much of it is just repetition, getting comfortable with both positioning and reacting to shots.

Here are some drills and games that cover the gamut, from the basics to the more advanced.

Goalie Wars

This is a fun game between two goalies, each defending a goal—regulation size or smaller, depending on your preference—with about 20 yards between them.

Each goalie is trying to score in the opposing goal by using any manner of distribution: punts, kicks from the ground, rolls, or throws. If scoring is too easy, push the goals farther back.

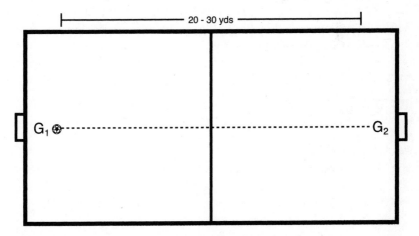

This is a great game for goalies to work on their shooting skills, too. You never know when they might need to play the field in a game.

Upsy-Daisy

Start with the goalie sitting on the ground. On his partner's signal, he must jump up and deal with a shot, then drop back to the ground. Line up 5 to 10 balls and do all the shots in a row, with the keeper going up and down each time. It's a great endurance drill and also works on proper handling.

Turnaround

Have the goalie stand on the goal line facing into the net. Line up five balls near the top of the penalty area. On a signal, the goalie must spin around and make a save immediately. Then he flips around and waits for the next signal.

This drill hones the goalie's reflexes as well as reinforces the value of a quick split-step before making a save.

MLS Shootout

Breakaways are a part of life for a goalie, so you might as well practice them. Have a line of players start about 30 yards from the goal and, one at a time, dribble in on the goalie one on one.

The rule is that the player must shoot the ball within five seconds or else the attempt is over. Goalies will quickly learn how important it is to narrow the angle in these situations.

WELL DONE!

In addition to narrowing the angle, a goalie should be prepared to slide out and grab the ball if a player dribbles too far in front of himself. It's a move that requires courage, but is often the best way to thwart a one on one chance.

The Least You Need to Know

♦ Being a goalie means being able to deal with a lot of pressure. It can be a lot of fun, but it's also not for everyone.

♦ What you do before the shot is as important as what you do after it. Proper positioning makes being a goalie a lot easier.

♦ Safety first. If you aren't sure that you can catch a ball, deflect it away from the goal so there's no chance it'll trickle in.

♦ Saving shots is only part of the job. Distributing the ball to teammates is how you contribute to your team's offense.

Part 4

Saturday in the Park

Game day: this is what playing soccer is all about. Even if you really, really love practicing (and how many actually do?), getting on the field and playing is the best part about soccer.

This part covers everything you need to know about playing a game. From what to eat in the morning to how early you should arrive at the field; from dealing with injuries to bringing the orange slices; from packing the equipment bag to being a volunteer assistant referee. Chapter 14 gives you a basic pregame primer.

Chapters 15 and 16 go over basic offensive and defensive strategies and movements, which will help you understand what's going on during a game. Chapter 17 is a simple guide for handling soccer injuries, while Chapter 18 is a mini-guide to being a model soccer spectator.

UNFORTUNATELY, THAT SEEMS TO BE THE ONLY WAY WE CAN GET MY MOM TO BEHAVE HERSELF DURING MY GAMES...

BARR

Chapter 14

Game Day Rites and Rituals

In This Chapter

- ◆ Handling pregame jitters
- ◆ Packing your game bag
- ◆ How to handle refreshment duty
- ◆ Getting enough rest
- ◆ What to do when you get to the field

It's 8 A.M. on a typical Saturday and the game is at 11 A.M. at the local park. Everybody's excited and questions abound:

> What do you eat? When do you leave for the game? What do you bring to the field? What if you're the parent who's supposed to bring the halftime snack?

Relax. Game day is supposed to be fun. Having a familiar game day routine can help quite a bit, and after you've got that down pat, everyone will be able to focus on just enjoying the game itself.

Getting the "Gameface" On

Every player handles the hours before a game differently. Some will be nervous and jumpy, bouncing around the kitchen and refusing to sit down; others will be nervous and stoic, sitting on the couch and staring straight ahead, or staying in their rooms until just before they're supposed to leave. Still others won't be nervous at all, maybe even to the point of looking disinterested.

All these reactions are normal and common, and there are a bunch more. Playing any sport, whether at the recreational level or in a more competitive situation, inspires emotions in people. There's no right way to get ready for a game, and the best way is simply whichever way feels most comfortable.

So what if you're dealing with a son or daughter who's completely overwhelmed by nerves? That's hardly unusual, too. Butterflies in the stomach are incredibly common, and the pregame is the hardest part. I always found the best approach was doing whatever I could to distract myself before the game started, because after I actually started playing, I forgot about being nervous—there just wasn't time with the game going on!

So talk about TV or your son's favorite baseball team or anything on the way to the game as long as it isn't about the game itself. Then when the game has started, your child will have forgotten all about how nervous he was an hour ago and hopefully that feeling will carry over to the following week's pregame, too.

Food for Thought

Sometimes a pregame meal feels like the worst idea ever. Particularly if you're nervous, the concept of putting anything into your stomach just doesn't compute. But you've got to eat, even if you feel as though your stomach is doing a rhythmic gymnastics routine already.

What to eat? Everyone has their own comfort foods, but the general idea with a pregame meal is this: put something in your stomach that will give you energy, but not weigh you down. Fatty breakfasts, such as donuts or sugary French toast probably aren't the best choices. You want something that has carbohydrates and can be easily digested: fruits, yogurt, and an English muffin are good places to start, and the ideal time to eat is about two hours before the game.

> **Throw-Ins**
>
> Former hockey star Wayne Gretzky had an interesting pregame routine. Gretzky wrote in his autobiography that he used to love to eat several hot dogs and drink a few Diet Cokes just before he went out onto the ice. Needless to say, although he turned out to be one of the greatest hockey players in history, that sort of pregame meal isn't recommended for everyone.

Don't look for an artificial energy boost, either. Sweets might give you a quick rush, but it'll be long gone by halftime, and then you'll be dragging. Caffeine is a bad choice, too, because it contributes to dehydration and can also irritate your stomach, making you have to go to the bathroom frequently. Not good.

I'm not a nutritionist so I'm not going to tell you that you shouldn't ever eat fast-food or anything like that, but try to avoid it on game day, and make sure you or your kid eats something more than just a granola bar or Egg McMuffin on the way to a game. As hard as it might be to get everything organized on the morning of a game, the pregame meal is very important. Every coach who's been around a while has seen a player get dizzy or even faint during a game, and usually it's because the player didn't have something to eat before spending her morning running all over the field.

Drink Up!

The best thing I can say about drinking water is this: do it. Do it a lot. Do it even more.

> **Yellow Card**
>
> Don't wait until you're already thirsty to start drinking water, and tell your kids the same thing. Thirst is the body's signal that it's *already* dehydrated—a situation that only gets worse the more a person continues to run around. Keep drinking water consistently during a game and don't let the body ever get to that point.

Kids in particular can easily get dehydrated. The best way to make sure that doesn't happen is to drink plenty of fluids before heading to the field. Oh, and soda doesn't count: anything with caffeine in it actually encourages dehydration, so that's counter-productive. You want to drink water or sports drinks (such as Gatorade). Make sure you have at least a few glasses of water before leaving for the game, and bring along a full water bottle (pack it with lots of ice, because the cubes will melt along the way) to drink during warm-ups and the game.

Remember: drink a lot of water. Then drink even more.

Pack Your Bags

It's a good idea for every soccer player to have an equipment bag. This makes it easier to keep everything together, cutting down on the "Mom, where's my left shinguard?" routine that will inevitably occur 20 minutes before it's time to leave. Keep cleats, shinguards, socks, shorts, and jerseys in the bag—after washing, fold them and put them back in there—and it'll make the morning of a game go that much easier.

What else should go in the game bag besides the basics? And what should be brought to the field? Each player has her own special additions to her game bag, but there are a few basics that most players carry.

Tape: A Player's Best Friend

About 20 minutes after any of my games in high school, the area around my team's bench would be littered with tiny white balls of used athletic tape. Just about everyone used tape somewhere on their uniform during a game, so afterward we would sit around and tear off the pieces and, occasionally, toss them at each other as we talked about the game. (Then we threw them in the trash—no litterbugs here!)

The point is that tape is very useful and all of us carried at least one or two rolls in our game bags. The few guys who didn't always seemed to be asking if they could borrow some. What can you do with tape? Plenty. Here's a few places soccer players find a strip or two of tape helpful:

- Around the ankles, for added support

- Above the shinguards—but not too tightly—to keep socks up

- Wrapped around the cleats, to keep laces from coming untied

- On the wrists of a goal-keeper, to keep gloves in place

> **WELL DONE!** Athletic tape doesn't necessarily have to be bought at soccer or sporting goods stores, where its price may be marked up. I used to buy my tape at the local pharmacy, where they sold it in packs of four or even eight rolls at a time. What a bargain!

Tape can also be useful in stabilizing an injury and can even be used to solve a uniform crisis. I've seen tape used to repair a ripped shirt or shorts, and to add a number to the back of a jersey when two players (somehow) showed up with the same number.

Long story short? Put some tape in your bag. It'll be worth it.

Braving the Elements

There's a rule in my local travel league that if the temperature is below 40 degrees, players are allowed to wear long pants during the game (typically they must wear shorts). This is a good, common-sense rule, and it's probably worth finding out if your league has a similar allowance.

Dealing with the weather can be tricky though, so it's best to pack some provisions in the game bag just to be safe. Here's a decent list of clothing items that might be worth having available to go in your bag. Obviously you can adjust the list depending on the season—feel free to leave the ski hat at home in July, for example:

- Turtleneck (preferably in same color as uniform jersey; if not, then black or white)

- Towels

- Water bottles

- Extra undershirts

- ◆ Hooded sweatshirt or fleece

- ◆ Sweatpants or training pants

- ◆ Flip-flops

- ◆ Knit hat

- ◆ Gloves (many players like "gripper" gloves that have tiny bumps on them to make it easier for throw-ins)

- ◆ Extra socks (to change at halftime if field is wet or rainy)

These are just suggestions, of course. Every player's bag is different. I had a teammate once who liked to change undershirts several times a day—he wore one during warm-ups, one during the first half, one during the second half, and then changed into another one after the game. Obviously that guy had a lot more t-shirts in his bag than most of us.

Are You on Snack Duty?

Many teams have rotating snack duty, which means that a different family is responsible for handling drinks and/or snacks for the players each week. Organized coaches will often put the names of the families responsible on the printed schedule of games each player receives, similar to this:

Date: May 20
Game: Larchmont vs. New Rochelle, 2 P.M.
Field: Flint Park
Snacks: Borden (drinks)/Weltman (oranges/postgame)

This way everyone knows when they've got to bring something to the game. If you're the one on duty this weekend, a good rule of thumb is to always make or bring more than you originally think you should. If there are 20 players on the team, bring 60 orange slices, just to be safe. You'd always rather have more than not enough.

Beverage Patrol

Many players bring their own water bottles, and some teams even have a cooler with four or five water bottles that all players can take a quick squirt from. If you're on beverage patrol, you're responsible for bringing sports drinks for halftime and postgame.

Yellow Card

It's very likely that there will be siblings of players at the games and they'll want a drink or an orange slice, too. Obviously you want to be accommodating to every kid, but you also have to make sure the players get the fluids they need during the game. It's just another reason to make sure you bring more food or drink than you think you might need.

Gatorade or Powerade are the standard drinks, and they come in a variety of flavors. If you don't know what most of the players like, it's probably best to bring several different kinds and—as with the oranges—better to bring one or two extra bottles instead of having too few.

You'll also want to bring a plastic trash bag, paper cups, and a cooler to keep the bottles in. About five minutes before halftime (and then again near the end of the game), start pouring the drinks into cups. It's helpful to have a tray to put the cups on, and some parents have found that using a cupcake sheet—which has indentations for each cupcake—is particularly useful because the cups are less likely to tip over.

As the players come off the field, offer the tray so they can take a cup, then grab a couple of the bottles and move around offering refills as the coach is talking to the players during the break. Have the trash bag ready when everyone is finished.

Orange Slices

The halftime orange slice is one of those soccer staples that has been around seemingly forever. It's cold, juicy, and refreshing, and it gives players a little burst of energy for their tired legs.

I always found the best (and neatest) way to prepare orange slices is to keep the peels on and simply cut the orange into four or six slices. Then put the slices into large plastic Tupperware containers or, if you prefer, plastic baggies. Keep them in a cooler or soft-pack if you have one during the game, and then offer them to the players at halftime.

Other Soccer Fare

Although the orange slice has been around almost as long as the soccer ball itself (or at least it feels that way), it's possible that you'll be part of a team that doesn't like oranges or is simply looking for a change of pace. Most fruit is a good substitute for a halftime snack, particularly apple slices or grapes.

WELL DONE! A postgame trip to the ice cream store or pizza place is almost always well-received and it shouldn't necessarily be tied to whether the team won or lost that day. If your child tried hard and the team lost anyway, there's still plenty of reason to go for a sugar cone with sprinkles.

If you're also responsible for bringing a postgame snack, you can go the fruit route as well, or consider something a little different. Individual bags of chips or pretzels are a good choice (because replenishing salt is always good after a game), or you could try some granola or trail mix.

There's also the donut route. Although it might not be the healthiest solution, when I was a young player I used to love it when a parent showed up with a box of Munchkins for the postgame; a little sugar always took the sting out of defeat or made a victory that much sweeter.

Time Is of the Essence

It's hard to find time to do anything sometimes, and that's no different when it comes to preparing for a soccer game. Everyone is afflicted: if you're a player, you might want to squeeze in some TV watching or homework (gasp!) before a game, and if you're a parent, it's tough not to try to run a few errands or get to a project before you head to the field. Balancing time is tricky.

There's nothing wrong with trying to multi-task, but playing soccer—especially if it's at any level above recreational—is a physically demanding task, so you want to make sure your body is completely ready to handle the rigors before you get into the game.

Sometimes that might mean putting off something the night before a game to make sure you get enough sleep or missing a TV show the afternoon after a game so you can get to that homework assignment. Sometimes, juggling off the field can be harder than juggling on it.

Typical Preparation Time

If a game starts at 10 A.M., most players would want to be up around 7:30 or so, particularly if they're the type who has a nervous stomach. That way, there's plenty of time to get down a pregame meal by 8, about two hours before kickoff.

Getting up a little earlier also means there's time to go through the game bag and double-check to make sure everything is in there—believe me, I've seen more than a few players show up to games without their jerseys, shinguards, and even cleats. Not having to rush makes it much easier to be sure you've got everything you'll need, plus any warm- or cold-weather additions, such as gloves or a hat, stuffed into the bag, too.

When you're sure you've got everything, change into your uniform (if you want, you can leave the shinguards and cleats off until you get to the field), then head out the door so you'll get to the field about 30 to 45 minutes before the game starts.

This way, you won't feel as though you're racing and you'll know for sure that you'll be ready to play when you arrive.

Soccer Sleep Deficits

Nobody ever gets enough sleep, right? With everything we have going on in our lives, it's pretty rare to find someone who feels as though they're always well-rested. But sleep is important, particularly for kids playing soccer.

Although many leagues substitute liberally and sometimes even build in extra timeouts, soccer is a sport that requires incredible endurance.

This isn't like baseball or golf or tennis, where there are lots of breaks in the action; soccer players start running at the beginning of the game and might not stop again until halftime. That's a lot to handle.

Getting a good night's rest before a game is critical, and the number of hours changes depending on a child's age. Experts seem to agree that 6- to 9-year-olds need around 9 to 10 hours of sleep a night, with 10- to 12-year-olds needing about an hour less. Teenagers should get between 8 and 9½ hours.

These suggestions might be tough to actually make happen, especially as kids get older and want to stay up to watch TV or talk on the phone or go see friends. I remember when I played club soccer as a high schooler, we often had our games at 9 A.M. on Sundays, which I always thought made no sense: didn't the schedulers know that teenagers like to go out on Saturday nights?

It didn't matter. That's when the games were so, even though it meant we had to stay in on some Saturdays, that's what we did. Trust me: playing soccer when you're tired is no fun at all.

Early Arrivals?

Arriving at a game early is always a good thing. The main reason is that it gives the player a chance to do a proper warm-up and stretch, and it also allows the coach to know for sure which players will be there as he makes out his lineup.

WELL DONE! There's nothing wrong with keeping one eye on the other team as you're warming up. By watching their players go through pregame drills, you might spot something they do particularly well (or poorly) that can benefit your team during the game. This sort of "scouting" is totally legal and can be very valuable!

A good rule of thumb for most youth games is to arrive about 30 minutes before kickoff. Park the car, head to the sidelines, and check-in with the coach or any teammates that are already there. This gives plenty of time for the player to drink some water and get into her pregame routine.

When I played, I always used this time to start thinking about a few skills I knew would be important to my team during that particular game—quick passing, maybe, or the need to cross the ball often in front of goal because the other team's goalie was inexperienced.

Even if you don't know the opponent very well, just thinking of a few basic fundamentals will get your mind in the right place for the game.

Quick Warm-Up

Stretching or "getting loose" is very important before a game—skipping it makes the risk of injury exponentially greater. Most teams have their own version of a routine they do before games as a group, and you should absolutely participate in that. It's probably not a bad idea to do your own stretching as well, though, particularly if it's a cold day and your muscles feel tight.

I always liked to start with a calf stretch because it felt as though that was my foundation. A simple way to stretch your calves is to put your hands on a goalpost or wall and step forward with one foot while keeping the heel of the other foot on the ground.

You should feel a stretching in the back of your leg; hold for a 10-count, then switch legs. Do this at least twice.

This is a great stretch for all players to do before practice and games. It'll loosen up your legs and get your foundation ready to run.

After the calves, loosen up the rest of your legs. Stretch your groins, quads, and hamstrings, then do some ankle rolls and neck rolls (see Chapter 17 for more detail on sample stretches for each part of the body).

You can probably run through your own stretching regiment in about 10 minutes. Then you'll be ready to start getting some touches on the ball as kickoff approaches.

Touches, Touches, Touches

A soccer ball feels different every day. Some days, it'll feel like you could dribble all day and never lose the ball; other days, it'll feel as though you're trying to kick a hard-boiled egg around the field.

That's the nature of any sport. The skills might be repetitive, but the challenge lies in consistency. That's why it's important to get as many touches as possible on the ball before the game; basically, you're reintroducing yourself to it every time. Wouldn't you rather have that happen before the whistle blows?

Every team I ever played for did some type of running together before the game started. Once around the field maybe, or twice, just to get the blood moving. It was universal.

> **Yellow Card**
>
> Some days a player just won't have it—whatever they do, they can't dribble the ball cleanly, can't get past a defender, can't keep possession. It happens to everyone. The best thing a player can do on these kinds of days is to adjust her expectations: look for the best available pass right away, for example, as opposed to trying to make a move on an opponent. The key is to do whatever possible to keep helping the team; better days will come soon enough.

Thing is, only a couple of the coaches I had told us to run with the ball and I'm not sure why that wasn't more common. It's a great way for a player to find out how smooth he feels with the ball at his feet that day, and it can only improve dribbling skills.

After their run, players should spend their remaining time before the game just getting as many touches on the ball as possible. Do some quick versions of 3 v. 1, with three players keeping the ball away from one defender by utilizing quick passes and constant movement. Just keep the ball rolling.

If there's a goal available, get the goalie some work by doing some shooting drills. Again, the idea is to simply put the foot on the ball, so have two players do one-touch passes for 10 yards or so before one shoots as they near the penalty area. The next pair should be right behind them and the line never stops. The more touches a player has before kickoff, the more comfortable he'll feel the first time the ball comes his way during the game.

The Least You Need to Know

- ◆ Nerves are natural, but a pregame meal is very important—even with a jumpy stomach.

- ◆ Pack a well-stocked game bag and you'll never have to worry about being unprepared for bad weather.

- ◆ Always bring more than you think you'll need, whether it's orange slices or drinks. Hungry and thirsty soccer players are a unique breed.

- ◆ There's no substitute for getting enough rest before a game.

- ◆ Arrive at the field early for the game—it'll give you plenty of time to warm up and stretch.

- ◆ Players should get as many touches on the ball as possible before kickoff so they feel comfortable with the ball during the game.

Chapter 15

Offensive Behavior

In This Chapter

- How players are arranged on the field
- How to tell if your offense is a good one
- Exploiting your opponent's weakness
- What offensive tactics work

There's a difference between knowing how to do something and actually doing it. Now that you've got the basics down for how to dribble, trap, pass, and shoot, the next step is putting it into action.

A free-flowing soccer attack can be a beautiful thing to watch ... or it can be ugly. Just as in other sports, there are several different ways to set up an offense and several different ways to score.

The Basic Types of Formations

Soccer teams set themselves up in a variety of *formations*, which refers to how many of each of the three types of players (forwards, midfielders, defenders) are placed on the field.

Each formation has three numbers, with each one indicating how many of that particular type of player should be on the field.

def•i•ni•tion

A **formation** is the way in which players are lined up on the field. They're usually given in numbers (4-3-3 or 3-5-2, say) with the order being defenders, then midfielders, then forwards.

Defenders are always given first, then midfielders, then forwards, and the numbers always add up to 10 (because that's how many players there are on the field, minus the goalie). As an example, a 4-3-3 formation means that, in this case, a team would be using four defenders, three midfielders, and three forwards.

There are no rules in soccer about how many of each type of player a team has to use. You can use as many forwards as you want, so long as there are only 10 players and the goalie on the field at any one time.

4-4-2

If a formation has four defenders, it's very rare to find all four spaced in a parallel line across the field. Typically, the defenders will be in a diamond, with two defenders on the wings (left fullback and right fullback) and two in the middle. The two in the middle are typically spaced with one ahead of the two wing defenders (called a *stopper*) and one behind them (called a *sweeper*).

def•i•ni•tion

If a team uses two center defenders in front of each other, the one in front is called the **stopper** and the one in back is the **sweeper**. If you can't remember which is which, remember that the stopper is the one who stops the attack before it gets close to the goal, and the sweeper is the one who sweeps up the messes near the net.

Teams that use this formation typically have very fast and very durable midfielders. The two inside midfielders handle their usual passing and supporting roles, while the outside midfielders spend most of the game running. Sometimes they're sprinting up to join the attack, then the next moment they're rushing back to help out on defense.

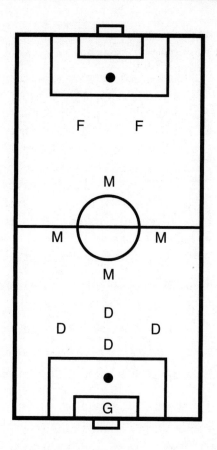

The 4-4-2 formation.

With the right group of players, this can be a very effective formation because the constant moving makes it difficult for the opponent to keep track of where all the players are going.

4-3-3

This is a pretty basic formation that you'll see at all levels of play. There are four defenders—most likely in the stopper/sweeper set-up we already covered—and the midfielders and forwards set up three across, with a center and two wings.

This is a well-balanced formation and one that most teams can use, regardless of personnel.

The 4-3-3 formation.

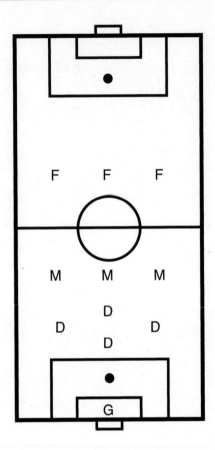

3-5-2

This is a more advanced formation and one you won't likely see until the players are older. It's a very fluid set-up, with three defenders—one sweeper and two wings—and five midfielders, who cover different areas of the field and are constantly switching. Then there are two forwards.

It's unlikely that a youth team would be using this set-up, but it's good to be able to recognize because you may see it if you attend a professional game. Watching the players work within the formation, especially the midfielders, offers a good example of how to play in different spaces on the field.

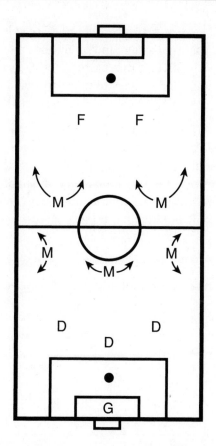

The 3-5-2 formation.

What Does a Good Offense Look Like?

There's no one right answer to this question, other than to say that a good offense looks like a group of players who score a lot of goals. Beyond sheer numbers, here are some ways to know if your offense is a quality one:

◆ **The ability to keep possession:** Are you constantly running after the other team? Does your team seem to give the ball away as soon as it gets it? Keeping possession means keeping control of the game. If you've got it, you're in much better shape than if you don't.

◆ **Completing passes:** The best teams are the ones that are able to string three, four, and five passes in a row, and oftentimes more than that. There's a purpose behind all that passing, too. The more you pass, the more the defenders have to move around and the more likely it is one of your players will be able to move into an open area and get a good chance on goal.

◆ **Communication:** It shouldn't be quiet on the field when your team has the ball. There should be voices coming from everywhere, as teammates let the person with the ball know where his support is coming from. *Back! Square! Overlap!* If you're not hearing much from your offense, it's probably not going to be very successful.

> **Throw-Ins**
>
> My favorite professional soccer team is Arsenal, a London-based club which plays in the English Premier League. The Gunners, as they're known, play a great possession game (often called "the beautiful game"). They literally pick the opposing team apart with their passes, constantly moving and refusing to be hurried, even if they're losing late in the game. Only when they sense an opening do they move forward and strike.
>
> It may not be the right strategy for every team, but it's right for them and that's why they stick with it.

These are just a few things to look out for in an offense. The truth, of course, is that if an offense is scoring goals, it probably shouldn't do too much tweaking!

Finding the Weak Spot

The more you watch soccer, the easier it will be for you to look at a team and determine its weak spot. Every team has one or more, even if they're small. The trick is figuring out how to turn your opponent's weakness into your advantage.

Sometimes it'll be easy to tell where the other team is lacking. Are all their defenders short? Maybe your team can take advantage by playing lots of high crosses and lofted balls? Do their midfielders seem slow? Maybe it's best to use lots of quick, one-touch passes to move up and down the field. Is their goalie struggling to hold on to shots during warm-ups? Try shooting from long range and then attacking the goal to pounce on the rebounds.

There's always something to try to exploit with the other team, and usually it'll be something you can identify pretty quickly. After you've done that, all you have to do is execute.

Yellow Card

In the same way that you might be able to find a weakness with the other team, your opponents can probably do the same with you. Use the different formations to try to hide your own weaknesses—using more defenders if your goalie is skittish, for example.

A Through Ball Attack

One example of an attack plan is to use the through ball, which is a pass designed to go in between (or through) the defenders into a space where a forward can catch up to it.

Teams that use this sort of plan typically have one or two forwards and midfielders who are adept at finding an open passing lane. The build-up is simple: they'll pass the ball around the midfield several times, and then try to thread a forward pass in between two of the fullbacks as the speedster whizzes by. If he gets to the ball, he's got a breakaway and a great chance to score.

A Chip-and-Run Attack

This offensive plan is similar to the through ball except that it involves lofting the ball through the air. This is a good plan if the other team has defenders who are poor at heading.

Teams that use this method don't spend too much time passing the ball on the ground in the midfield. Typically, if they get possession, they'll quickly look upfield and loft the ball into open space—frequently down the sidelines—where they'll then try to move in on goal.

Outside-In Attack

Moving through the middle of the field can be difficult. Why? Because that's where most of the players are! Consequently, many of the goals you see in professional games come from the wings, when attackers dribble the ball deep into the attacking zone and then cross the ball to the middle for a header or a quick shot into the net.

This outside-in approach is particularly effective against teams who have slower left and right fullbacks. If your forwards can get behind them with the ball, they'll be able to take it toward the end line before cutting it back into the middle of the field near the goal.

Tactics That Work

If you're not coaching a team, it's probably not a good idea to get too involved in discussing their gameplans. That said, there are some general offensive tactics that are pretty universal in terms of success.

These are basic soccer concepts that certainly don't guarantee victory if they're done well, but they'll probably make the game a lot more enjoyable if a team is able to incorporate them.

Finding Space

You know how aggravating it can be to be stuck in traffic? Cars all around you on every side and you can't move anywhere? That's what you want to avoid on the soccer field.

Finding space should be a perpetual goal for a soccer player, regardless of whether she's a forward, midfielder, or defender. If you've got the ball, you should be looking for open space because that's where you want to pass the ball; if your teammate has the ball, you should be looking for open space because that's where you'll be in the best position to receive a pass.

Many of the drills we've explained in earlier chapters involve finding space, and it's easier to do when you're inside a coned-off grid. During a game, however, it's a little harder.

Sometimes finding space just means stepping into a teammate's line of vision. Sometimes it means slipping behind an opponent. Sometimes it means going all the way out to the sideline, or even circling back behind a teammate to give them support.

What's the benefit of space? The biggest advantage is simple: your opponent can't steal the ball if he's not near you. By finding space, you're making it more likely you'll be able to make a successful dribbling move, pass, or shot. The other benefit is that finding space keeps your opponents running. If they're chasing you around all game, they'll be pretty tired when it comes time for them to have the ball.

WELL DONE!

It can feel pretty crowded on the soccer field sometimes, especially in younger-age games. If you're struggling to get the ball, try doing the opposite of what you'd think—instead of going toward the ball, look for any space away from it and go there. You may find that you're a better target for a pass that way.

Quick Passes

Back and forth, back and forth, back and back and forth and forth. Sometimes that's what a good passing team can look like: one pass after another after another. It's pretty to watch, especially if each pass is moving crisply and each trap is steady and secure.

WELL DONE!

Here's an advanced move to try on the field that isn't hard at all. The next time your team is moving the ball with quick passes, think about trying a "dummy run," which basically just means acting as if you're going to receive a pass but letting it go past you. If a defender is running close to you expecting you to get the ball and you let it go, there's likely to be an opening right behind you where a teammate can pick up the ball and go for goal.

When a team has the ball in its offensive end of the field, quick passes are sometimes the only way to break through the line of fullbacks. A well-executed wall pass will often spring a forward in for a chance on goal, and frequently players—in the name of finding space—will make short runs through the penalty area and back out, getting the ball and giving it up quickly for a teammate to take a shot.

There's no set way to use quick passes as an attacking scheme, and each offense that utilizes quick passing is sort of like a snowflake in that every combination is different. One technique that often works, however, is to have a player near the penalty area with his back to the goal. He can receive a pass while shielding the ball with his body, and then quickly dump the ball off to another teammate running nearby for a shot on net.

The Long Ball

I remember playing against a few teams that just refused to dribble the ball. They were all about the long pass and as soon as they gained possession of the ball they just let it go, a big lofted kick down the field that they hoped would land where their forwards could get to it.

As a goalie, I quickly recognized that this style of play put the defenders and me under constant pressure. There was no rest: every time my team turned the ball over, I could count on a long ball heading in my direction within seconds.

For some teams, this sort of plan works well. A team with quick forwards and strong-footed fullbacks will be able to keep their opponents on the defensive all game, but it also doesn't take much work to deal the long balls if you've got defenders who can head the ball and a goalie who is capable of making sure everyone is covered.

Still, the long ball attack can be effective, especially at younger age levels. It just takes a lot of running and the willingness to kick a lot of passes that don't work out, in anticipation of the one that might lead to a great scoring chance.

The Least You Need to Know

- There are a variety of different formations, but all of them involve numbers and the order of the numbers is always defenders, then midfielders, then forwards.

◆ Successful offenses in soccer don't all look the same. Sometimes scoring comes from short, quick passing on the ground, and sometimes it comes from long, lofted passes in the air.

◆ Try and identify your opponent's weakness on defense, then figure out how to exploit it to your advantage on offense.

◆ Finding open space is always important. Without it, any offense will be stifled as though it's in gridlock.

Chapter **16**

Getting Defensive

In This Chapter

- ◆ What it means to mark up
- ◆ How to tackle
- ◆ The 10 simple rules to good defense
- ◆ Understanding the life of a defender

If you stand in front of a group of young soccer players and say, "Everyone who wants to play offense, go to my left, and everyone who wants to play defense, go to my right," it's very likely that in about two seconds you'll have every single player standing on your left. In other words, playing defense isn't the most popular job in the whole world.

But defense is a critical part of the game, and even if it seems like a less exciting task than scoring goals, it's as important—if not more important—to whether a team wins. Defenders are the heart of the team. Without a strong defense, a team has no backbone.

The Basics

There are times when a defender can and should move up and be part of his team's attack, but typically fullbacks spend most of their time during a game thinking one of two things:

- ◆ What can I do to take the ball away from the other team?
- ◆ What can I do to make sure the other team doesn't score?

These are the overriding premises behind good defending, and the core concept behind both is *marking* an opponent well.

def•i•ni•tion

> **Marking** is the soccer word for covering an opponent.

Marking is the soccer word for "covering," or doing whatever you can to make sure the attacker isn't able to score. At its essence, marking a player means keeping yourself between them and the goal—if you're able to do that, it's going to be pretty hard for them to get the ball in the net.

Marking Off the Ball

If you've got a good (and loud) goalie behind you, you'll often hear her calling out numbers and locations for where you should be marking as the other team tries to move its attack down the field.

"Sam, watch 5 on the left!" means I should look left and find no. 5 on the opposing team, and mark them. So how do I do that? Marking a player who doesn't have the ball isn't the same as marking a player who does. In this case, the key is making sure you're able to keep the player in front of you (so he doesn't break in on goal and get a pass), as well as keeping an eye on where the ball is so you can readjust your defense if another assignment develops that's more important (an attacker gets by a teammate and you have to rush over and help out, for example).

An important element of marking off the ball is keeping your body open to the field; if a player is on the left wing, for example, you want to be facing them with your body angled so that you're looking at them out of your left eye. That way, you can see what they're doing but also see the rest of the play out of the corner of your right eye.

WELL DONE! Keeping an eye on the attacker and an eye on the rest of the play can be tough if you're only comfortable running forward. A defender who's confident running backward and in a side-step fashion will always have an advantage because he'll be able to see everything and keep moving all at once.

If the player you're marking doesn't have the ball, you don't have to be up close to him. In fact, it's better to lay off a little, so there's less of a chance your opponent can sprint past you. Give the player a little space, and it'll be much easier for you to keep track of his movements.

Marking On the Ball

So let's say you're doing a great job marking off the ball: your opponent is making runs and you're staying with him, but suddenly he steps back and receives a pass a little outside your penalty area. You're in front of him and now he's got the ball. What do you do?

♦ **Close the player down:** This means getting a little closer. You'll hear coaches yelling, "close him down, close him down!" all the time, and the point of doing it is that it will be much, much harder for a player to take a shot if a defender is near him. If there's lots of room, the player might decide to take a crack at goal from wherever he is, catching the goalie off-guard. Step up so you're a few feet away, and that option is eliminated.

♦ **Approach at an angle:** In other words, don't run at the attacker straight on. First, it makes it much easier for him to get around you, and second, it doesn't force him in any one direction. Instead, you want to approach at an angle, preferably one that will push the attacker away from the middle of the field. Why? Because the middle of the field is where the goal is. If the attacker moves toward the outside, it's harder for him to have a good look at the goal.

♦ **Stay balanced:** The basic defending stance is one with knees bent, body angled so the attacker is being pushed to the outside, with one foot slightly in front of the other (that way there's less chance the attacker can slip the ball between your legs). Keep your weight evenly distributed between your feet, and keep your head down, eyes on the ball.

Keep one foot in front of the other, stay low, and keep your balance even. This puts you in the best position to make a successful tackle and steal the ball.

After you've done these three things, you'll be in the correct position to try and *tackle* the attacking player. And no, that doesn't mean laying them out—it just means making a play in which a defender takes the ball away from his opponent.

Tackling (But Nobody Gets Hurt)

There are several ways to tackle in soccer, and it's up to the defender to pick the best one to use at the right time. Slide tackling is the technique that is most well-known, mostly because it looks like the most exciting—after all, who doesn't love sliding?

def•i•ni•tion

Nobody gets slammed to the ground in a soccer **tackle;** it just means one player has taken the ball away from an opponent.

But while slide tackling can be very effective, it's also far from the only way to succeed as a defender. In fact, the other tackling techniques are almost always a better option, if only because you don't end up on the ground (and out of the play) afterward.

Stepping In

If you've closed down the opponent and are in a good, balanced position, all that's left is to take the ball. The basic tackle involves simply stepping in and blocking the ball with the inside of one of your feet.

When do you pounce? The two best chances are when the attacker looks up to find a teammate that she's going to pass the ball to, or when she starts to make a dribbling move.

To take the ball, keep your head down and step in with your body so that your hip is nearly pushing into the defender as the inside of your foot contacts the ball. You don't want to lunge—that's easier for the attacker to avoid. You want to move smoothly and swiftly, and establish your possession so that the attacker can't move in a different direction.

Shoulder-to-Shoulder

Soccer is a physical game and, even though there are plenty of things you're not allowed to do to take the ball away, one act that *is* legal is a shoulder-to-shoulder bump.

Basically, that means that if you're coming up alongside a player who has the ball, you're allowed to step in and move them off as long as the contact is with your shoulder against their shoulder.

If it's in their back or chest, that's not allowed; one shoulder to another, however, is perfectly acceptable. The key to pulling off this kind of tackle is to get your shoulder out in front of the attacker's shoulder and use that leverage to push the attacker away.

Then use your outside foot—the one farthest away from the ball—to move the ball in the other direction. Why the outside foot? If you use the inside foot, it'll be much easier for the attacker to steal the ball back.

The shoulder-to-shoulder tackle is a legal way to take the ball. Just make sure you keep your elbow down and your shoulder in front of the opponent so you can maintain leverage.

Slip 'n' Slide

The slide tackle is the best-known tackle, but as we said before, it should really be used as a last resort. If you slide tackle and miss, you'll be on the ground and your team will be playing down one defender until you get up and start running again. That's a big risk to take.

> **Yellow Card**
>
> Slide tackling successfully is about timing. If you mis-time the slide, you'll either miss the ball and player completely, or slide directly into the player, which will almost surely be called a foul and could result in a yellow card. Also, *never* slide tackle a player from behind. If you do, there's a good chance you'll injure the player and get yourself a red card.

You can slide tackle on either side of your body, but let's imagine you're going to try to take the ball with your right leg. Here's what you do:

1. Get low to the ground immediately and turn to the side. You want the sliding surface to be your left hip.

2. Bend your left leg about 90 degrees and tuck it underneath your right leg.

3. Extend your right leg out as far as it goes and keep your toe pointed.

4. Contact the ball with your instep, right on the laces of your cleat. If you want to try and keep possession, hook the ball with the instep; if you want to just knock it away, pop the ball with the instep and try to send it to safety.

5. Using your left hand, push yourself back up to your feet.

Done correctly, the slide tackle is a valuable weapon and one that can be very effective in quickly stopping an opponent's attack.

> **WELL DONE!**
>
> Depending on the age of your child, certain leagues may have rules that prohibit slide tackling altogether. Make sure you check with the coach or an official to find out if slide tackling is allowed.

Ten Simple Rules to Being a Good Defender

Now that you know the basics of marking and the different types of tackling, here are 10 simple rules to putting it all together on the field:

1. **Keep the middle clear:** The sides of the field are safe, the middle is dangerous. Try and shade defenders to the sides and, if you get the ball and don't know where to pass it, kick it to the sides, not the middle. There's much less chance of giving up a goal there.

2. **Don't lunge:** Don't be tempted by a slick-dribbling attacker. Keep your eye on the ball and, when the time is right, swoop in for a tackle. Don't just awkwardly jump in right away.

3. **Talk:** There's no substitute. Call out where open players are and, if a teammate gets the ball, remind him to "Clear to the side!"

4. **Move out:** If one of your teammates steals the ball and starts to pass it up the field, start running upfield, too. Not only will you be in a better position to support your team's attack, you'll leave the other team's players in an offside position behind you.

5. **Listen to the goalie:** They have the best view of the field and can tell you where you should be going. Don't argue. Just go.

6. **Wait for help:** Sometimes the best defensive play is to just stay in front of an attacker and slow them up. This is often called *jockeying*, and if it's done successfully, it'll give your teammates time to run back and help you tackle.

7. **Play the ball:** If you get stuck in a two on one situation, always stick with the man who has the ball. If you can force him to make a decision (to either pass or dribble), you've done your job. Stay with the ball and let your teammates hustle back to pick up the other player.

8. **Stay balanced:** If you're the right fullback, don't run all the way over to the left side of the field. Stay in your area (unless you're the only defender between the attacker and the goal), and keep an eye out for attackers lurking nearby. Those are the players you should be marking.

9. **Be committed:** When you go for a tackle, you should do it with the intention of winning the ball every time. Don't try to tackle if you're not sure you can get the ball. If you have doubt, just jockey and wait for help.

10. **Get it out!:** Kicking the ball out of bounds should never be a bad thing for a defender. If your goal is under attack and you can get a foot on the ball, just kick it away as hard as possible. A throw-in is better to give up than a goal.

Obviously there are more complex defensive strategies that coaches may employ, but these basic rules are applicable to just about any situation a defender might face during a game.

Specialty D

Playing good defense during regular play is a free-flowing phenomenon, but there will be times when special situations come up and the defense has to get very organized in a very short amount of time.

Most of these situations come during restarts—a foul or a corner kick, for example. The key to all of them is to listen—listen to what the coach is saying and listen to what the goalie is saying. They'll be calling out directions that will help you keep the other team off the scoreboard.

The Wall

If the opposing team is given a free kick somewhere near the penalty area, you'll likely be told to be part of the *wall*, which is a line of defenders standing next to each other to help obscure part of the goal.

The rules say that defenders must be at least 10 yards away from the ball on free kicks, and the referee may tell you exactly where you're allowed to stand.

Listen to the goalie: he'll call out how many defenders should be in the wall, and he'll position the wall left or right. One of the players in the wall should keep looking at the goalie as the free kick is being set up, so that he can follow the goalie's directions (*"Two steps left! One step right!"*).

When the wall is set, don't lock arms with the other defenders (so you'll be free to run after the kick is taken), and keep your eyes open. If the ball comes at you, try to deflect it forward and to the side, and then run back into your normal position.

 Throw-Ins

You'll often see male players covering their groin area with their hands when they are lined up in the wall and who can blame them? If you want to do this, go ahead—few referees would call a handball if the ball should hit your hand there!—but just be ready to get moving as soon as the kick is taken.

Corner Kicks

Most teams want to have one defender guard either post on a corner kick. If you're guarding the near post, be on guard for a low corner kick right at you that's targeted for the goal box. Step up and boot it back in the direction it came (not the middle, remember?).

If you're covering the back post, be aware of the high floating ball into your area, but don't be tempted. Trust your teammates to mark the attackers and stay at the post until the ball is clear. Your job is to be a last line of defense; I can't count the number of times I've seen an attacker head the ball toward goal off a corner kick and the defender covering the back post is there to kick it away and save a goal.

WELL DONE! Defensive heading is a big part of dealing with corner kicks (and any kind of lofted crosses from the wing). The key is to try and head the ball back where it came. If it comes from the right, head it back in that direction. That's always preferable to heading it across the middle of the field—where an attacker might be waiting with an easy shot on goal.

If you're not covering one of the posts, try to stay inside of the player you're marking and then attack the ball if it comes in your direction. If it doesn't, stay close to your mark and be wary of loose balls being scuffed around in the area. They can be dangerous.

Penalty Kicks

More often than not, a penalty kick results in a goal. After all, it's a free shot from 12 yards out—a tough situation for any goalkeeper.

But your job as a defender is to make sure that if your goalie does save the shot, you're there to knock the ball away and keep the attacking team from scoring off the rebound. This means you want to position yourself just outside the penalty area (the rules say you must wait there until the kick is taken), but then rush in as soon as the kicker strikes the ball, so you'll be ready to deal with a deflection off the goalie or the post. Don't just sit back and watch the kick being taken. Be ready to get in there when your goalie comes through with a big save!

Basic Defensive Schemes

It seems as though there are a million different defensive schemes in football and all of them have pretty funny names: the Cover 2, the Dime Package, or Prevent. Soccer coaches can come up with some complex strategies for defense, too, but there are two basic ways to defend: man-to-man and zone.

Man-to-Man Defense

This is the simplest method of defense: each player is responsible for a corresponding player on the other team, and that's the person they cover. For young players, it's an easy-to-understand strategy, though it can present its own issues when players lose track of their mark.

Still, man-to-man can be a good strategy to use if a team has one or two very good defenders and wants to blanket the one or two best attackers on the other team. The biggest obstacle is making sure that players are comfortable with the idea of leaving their own men to help out if a teammate gets beat by his mark.

Zone Defense

Zone defense is exactly what it sounds like. Each defender is responsible for an area on the field, and when an attacker comes into that area, the defender must mark him. This strategy requires a lot more communication between defenders, particularly if a team has multiple attackers in a particular area (thus forcing defenders to temporarily leave their zones to compensate). Usually the zones are divided as you'd expect (right fullback handles the right side of the field, left fullback the left, etc.), and if there's a sweeper in the formation then he is responsible for roaming to wherever help is needed.

Each player is responsible for marking the attackers in her zone, though communication is important. If one zone is flooded with attackers, everyone needs to shift over to compensate.

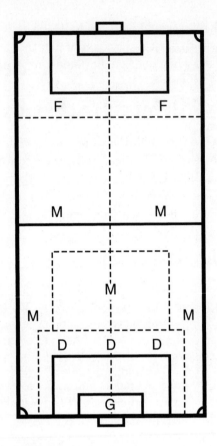

The Life of the Defender

There's no one type of player who fits the mold as a defender. Some are big, some are small, some are fast, some are slow; as a goalie, I always liked the ones who were confident and aggressive. They were the ones who usually made my job a little less stressful.

Being a defender means being okay with not getting the same kind of attention as attackers. Everyone loves to score goals and everyone loves a goal-scorer. Playing defense is a different kind of job. There won't be as much praise (except from your coach and your goalie) and your mistakes can be a lot more noticeable if they end up as goals for the other team. That's a different kind of pressure for a player to handle.

The rewards are terrific though. As great as it feels to score a goal, the feeling of containing a good offensive team and keeping a *clean sheet*, or shutout, is unmatchable. The old saying about football and basketball applies to soccer, too: offense wins games, but defense wins championships.

def•i•ni•tion

A **clean sheet** is another way of saying that a team allowed no goals in a game. It's also called a shutout.

The Least You Need to Know

♦ Don't rush to tackle the ball. If you're not sure you can get the ball away from the attacker, jockey and wait for help.

♦ A slide tackle may look cool, but it should be a last resort. Going to the ground means you're leaving your team without a defender.

♦ Listen to the goalie. He's got the best view of the field and can tell you who you need to be marking.

♦ Defenders don't get the glory that forwards do, but they're just as important to a team's success and may be under even more pressure.

Chapter 17

Joy and Pain

In This Chapter

- Prepping your body to avoid injuries
- Identifying common ailments
- Basic treatments
- Getting over tough losses

Injuries are a part of any sport, and soccer has its share. Most are minor—a cramp, a mild sprain, a cut or two or three—and it's common for many younger-age teams to make it through an entire season without anyone getting hurt.

Still, you always want to be prepared so it's a good idea to have an idea of what most soccer injuries look and feel like—that way you can make sure no one has to spend any more time on the sidelines than absolutely necessary.

How to Prevent Injuries

Instead of jumping right in and describing what a sprained ankle feels like (not good, by the way), it's worthwhile to spend a few minutes talking about what players can do to make it less likely they'll get hurt in the first place.

The key to warding off many injuries is properly preparing the body for the game; in other words, a comprehensive stretching routine.

Some coaches and teams do a good job with this, but if yours doesn't, here's a quick full-body stretching sequence that should get you warmed up for action:

◆ **Calf stretch:** Step forward with right knee bent and put hands on right thigh; keep left foot down and feel left calf stretch. Then reverse.

◆ **Hamstring stretch:** Sit with both feet together extended out in front of you; tuck chin to chest and reach forward with both hands as far as possible. Should feel stretch in back of legs.

◆ **Quadriceps stretch:** Stand and pull one foot up behind you with knee fully bent (hold teammate or wall for balance). Then switch legs.

◆ **Groin stretch:** Sit with soles of feet touching directly in front of you with knees off to side; lean forward and push down gently on knees with elbows.

◆ **Back stretch:** Stand and stretch both arms behind back while pushing chest out; hold for a few seconds and then release.

◆ **Neck stretch:** Stand with hands on hips and rotate neck clockwise for 10 seconds slowly; then reverse to counter-clockwise.

◆ **Ankle stretch:** Stand with hands on hips and rotate each ankle clockwise for 15 seconds slowly; then reverse to counter-clockwise. Switch ankles and repeat.

WELL DONE!

A lot of attention is (rightfully) paid to the warm-up, but doing a proper "cool-down" after the game is often overlooked. While drinking some water and listening to the coach after the game, make sure you do many of these same stretches for at least 5 to 10 minutes to make sure your muscles don't cramp up and constrict. It'll also reduce your postgame soreness.

These are just a few of the stretches you can and should do before practices and games. It's also good to do some light jogging and get some easy touches on the ball before you play, which is why it's important to arrive at the field with enough time to properly prepare before a game. It doesn't guarantee you won't get hurt, but it certainly makes it much less likely.

Soccer Triage

So it happened. Someone is crying or someone is holding their side (or leg or elbow or hip), and now you've got to figure out what's wrong with them. Sideline diagnoses are an acquired skill, but most of it is just common sense. The best advice is to always be cautious: obviously you don't want to keep a kid (or yourself) out of the game if he's not that hurt, but there's also the risk of aggravating an injury if he returns to action too quickly.

Be safe. Make sure you're confident you know what an injury is before you decide it's not serious enough to keep out of action. If you're not sure what an injury is, don't go back on the field. Relax, get it checked out by someone who knows, and go from there. There will always be another game to play.

Sprains and Strains and Tears

These are pretty common injuries in soccer (or any sport involving running), particularly for ankles. If you hear someone say they "rolled an ankle" that's another way of saying they sprained the ligaments that hold the joint together.

Some sprains are mild and take only a few days to feel all better. More serious sprains can be season-ending if the muscle fibers tear completely, and you'll

Yellow Card

Tearing an ACL, or anterior cruciate ligament, is a serious knee injury which statistics show is more common in females. Why? The most common explanation seems to be that women land with a straighter leg than men do, which minimizes the shock absorption that's typically offered by the quad muscle.

know if the injury is that bad because it will be very difficult to walk, much less run or play soccer.

At the worst end of the spectrum are ligament tears, which can occur in a knee or Achilles' tendon. These are major injuries which will require lengthy rehabilitation and physical therapy.

Pulled Muscles

Remember what I said earlier about the importance of stretching? Pulled muscles are typically what happen if you don't stretch well enough. Pulled muscles feel like what they're called—a stretching of a muscle, whether it's your quad, hamstring, or groin—and there isn't much to do in terms of treatment other than resting. That's why the best way to handle pulled muscles is to do whatever you can to avoid them by stretching properly before a game or practice.

Throw-Ins

One way to figure out if an injured player can go back into the game is to use the "five-minute rule." Basically, if a player feels better after five minutes of rest—her ankle has stopped hurting and she can run again, for example—then she's allowed back. If there's still a lot of pain after five minutes, it's probably best to keep her on the sidelines.

Cuts and Bruises

With all the kicking and sliding that goes on during a soccer game, it's no surprise that many players end up black-and-blue on their shins and knees, as well as the occasional scrape or wound.

Children especially may be frightened if they start bleeding, but quick action can get them cleaned up and back on the field. If you're going to handle a cut, make sure to wear latex gloves (should be in any first-aid kit), and apply pressure to the wound to stop the bleeding. Then clean the cut with an alcohol swab or towelette and cover it securely with a bandage.

Cramps

With all the running that goes on during a game, cramps are a natural and common occurrence. Cramps will often appear in a player's side or stomach and feel similar to a "stitch" or some other dull pain. If this happens, a quick substitution should do the trick; a few minutes of rest, a drink of water, and some controlled breathing will have the player ready to go back on to the field.

Sometimes you'll also encounter muscle cramps—a calf cramp, for example—which can be very painful, too. To deal with these, try to massage the area where the cramp is located and then stretch that particular muscle out (see the previous section) for several minutes. The cramp should slowly dissipate.

Breaks and Fractures

These are more serious injuries and, especially in the case of a broken bone, the player will know that he's seriously hurt. Obviously this calls for a trip to the hospital for x-rays and tests.

Fractures can be more difficult to detect. As a goalie, I suffered hairline fractures to my thumb on two different occasions, and both times I wasn't totally sure at first how badly I was hurt. If sharp pain and swelling lingers or makes it difficult to rotate or flex a limb, it's probably worth having a doctor check you out. You don't want to take the chance you'll make a tiny fracture even worse.

Head Injuries

Head injuries don't happen that often in soccer but there is a risk, especially when players go to head the ball and clash heads with an opponent or teammate.

Yellow Card

Whenever your child joins a new team, you should always check to see if the coach (or one of his assistants) is trained in CPR. You should also make sure that the coach has contact numbers (cell, office, etc.) for you and anyone else responsible for your child with him at every practice and game. That way if something happens, you or your family can be easily reached.

Even though most head injuries may turn out to be not serious, all of them should be treated seriously at first. Suffering a *concussion*, or blow to the head that reaches the brain, can be minor or major. Here are some signs that you should probably contact a doctor or go to the emergency room:

◆ Vomiting

◆ Vertigo

◆ Unmatched dilation of pupils

◆ Numbness in body

◆ Inability to walk or keep balance

◆ Unconsciousness or fainting

◆ Inability to speak

◆ "Seeing stars" or hazy vision

def•i•ni•tion

A **concussion** is a head injury in which there is a temporary loss of brain function. Concussions can range from mild to serious.

Most of the time a concussion ends up with a player just having a bit of a headache the next day, but it's still important to be absolutely sure that there isn't a crack in the skull or a more serious injury. Especially at younger ages, don't trust the player to say he's okay; if he suffered a head injury, keep him on the sidelines for the rest of the game.

When to Go to the Hospital

No game is more important than a player's health, so whether the team will win or lose should never be a factor in deciding whether or not to go to the hospital after an injury.

There's also no manual that tells you exactly what to do in every situation. A lot of it is just common sense: if a wound is bleeding profusely and the flow can't be stopped, go to the hospital. If a bone is protruding or a player literally can't stand or walk, go to the hospital. If a player loses consciousness or is having trouble breathing, go to the hospital.

Never be embarrassed to have a player, especially a child, checked out by a trained physician. Yes, they're probably going to be fine. But why take a chance?

Routine Maintenance

Home treatment of minor injuries is a pretty basic part of being a soccer player. Most of the time, the easiest way to treat a nagging injury—a slight muscle strain, a bruise, anything, really—is with the RICE method. What's that mean? It's an acronym which stands for:

1. **R**est: Whatever the injury, stay off it for a little while. If you hurt your ankle, try to avoid walking or running on it. Take it easy. Then, after a few days, try some light exercise to see how it feels. When you feel no pain, you can return to practice.

2. **I**ce: Whenever you injure a part of your body, blood rushes to that area which is why swelling occurs. Applying ice constricts the blood vessels and reduces the swelling. It'll also make the healing time quicker. Ice should be applied as often as possible in the first day or two after an injury, but never for more than 20 minutes at a time (to prevent frostbite). Also, don't put ice directly on your skin; put a wet cloth between the ice and injured area.

3. **C**ompression: Wrapping an area that's been injured will keep the blood flow to that area down, reducing swelling. It also provides more support to a tender joint or muscle, making it less likely that you'll re-aggravate an injury. Many players continue to wrap an ankle or a thigh that they've tweaked, for example, even several weeks later, just to be sure they've got as much support in the area as possible.

4. **E**levation: When you're resting, you want to make sure you get the injured area above your heart—this will also limit the blood pumping to that area and keep swelling down. If you're nursing an ankle or knee injury, keep that leg on a pillow above you as you lie down whenever possible.

RICE is a pretty basic treatment method for injuries, and in most cases it'll get the job done. If you've been doing RICE for several days and the injury doesn't seem to be improving, it's time to have a doctor or physical therapist take a look. There are a number of other rehabilitation techniques that are very effective, and a physician will be able to identify the right things to do to deal with your specific injury.

Heady Stuff

Not all injuries are physical. Sometimes the biggest hurdle for a player to get over is a mental one, and those obstacles can be as tough—or even tougher—than a cut or a scrape or a bruise.

As a parent, the first thing you need to do is figure out *exactly* what is bothering your child. It may take some digging, particularly if you get a lot of "nothing" and "it's fine" from him, and even if it's clear he's holding something back. After you've figured out the issue, then you can do your best to try and address it.

Getting Over Being the Goat

As a goalie, I always felt some level of responsibility for a loss, particularly if I hadn't played my best game. Trust me, it's hard to get over it if you don't play well; that's just part of playing.

Two things I always tried to keep in mind though, especially when I was younger, were:

- **The ball had to get past 10 other people before it got past me.** I didn't use that as a cop-out, because there were times when I should have made a save that I didn't.

    But thinking about that fact did make me feel better about the idea that soccer is a team game, and even if I made a mistake, it wasn't *just* me that lost the game: the forwards could have scored more; the midfielders could have passed better; the defenders could have kept the ball further away from the goal. Everyone plays a part in a win and everyone plays a part in a loss. That's the beauty of a team sport.

- **Leave it at the park.** This is hard to do sometimes, particularly if it's an elimination or tournament game. But I always tried to get all my anger or frustration out while I was at the field or on the ride home. By the time I got home, I tried my best to let it go.

Obviously these thoughts don't always make it easy to get over a big mistake or a tough loss. Sometimes it just takes a little time. The important thing to do is to get back out and start playing again—if there isn't a practice or game for a week, just kick the ball around as soon as possible. The best medicine for a rough game is often getting back into the game itself.

WELL DONE! Most coaches do a good job at reminding players that soccer is a team sport, but some will get into the blame game. Keep an eye on how your child's coach responds to a tough loss; if he or she is putting too much blame on a particular player, that may be a big factor in the child's emotional state.

Building Self-Confidence

Athletes can often fall into a pattern of allowing how they play to define how they feel about themselves, and as a parent, that's something you want to be on the lookout for.

However badly a player may feel after she has a bad game, it's not an indication that she's a bad person (or even a bad player!). Although kids may not want to hear it, reminding them that everyone makes mistakes is important. No one should be defined by what they do on the field—good or bad, a person is much bigger than what she does when she's wearing cleats.

The Least You Need to Know

- ◆ Many soccer injuries are preventable by doing a proper warm-up before the game.
- ◆ Don't ever rush players back onto the field if they've been hurt, especially if they've suffered a head injury.
- ◆ RICE is a good way to treat most injuries; if it doesn't help after a few days though, it's time to see a doctor.
- ◆ Getting over a tough loss is difficult, but no mistake on the field should ever make a player feel like a bad person.

Chapter 18

Stalking the Sidelines

In This Chapter

- ◆ How to be a linesman
- ◆ The best kind of fan
- ◆ Knowing when your child has had a "good game"

Coaches do their best to make practicing soccer fun, but nothing compares to playing in a game. All the skills you've tried to hone are now on display, and playing a part in helping your team win is an experience that simply can't be matched.

Game day can be just as rewarding if you're a parent watching your child play. You want to cheer for them, support them, and encourage them, but you also want to do it in the right way. In other words, you don't want to be a sideline terror. Remember: the players are the ones on the field. They're the ones that everyone should be watching.

If You're Asked to Be a Linesman

Some leagues have enough officials that there will always be a referee and two linesmen (actually called "assistant referees") assigned to every game. In many places, however, there will only be one neutral referee working the game and each team will have to provide an assistant referee. So what happens if you, as the parent of a player, are asked to do this job? First of all, don't worry—it's not hard labor. Here's what you do:

1. Meet with the referee and take a flag from him. He'll ask you to work on one side of the field (probably the side your team's bench is on).

2. When the game starts, move up and down the sideline so that you're in the vicinity of where the ball is located.

3. When the *entire ball goes over the entire sideline or goal line*, raise the flag straight up in the air. Most of the time, this is all the referee will want you to do. If he specifically asks you to point a direction indicating which team should get the throw-in, you can do so. If you're not comfortable doing that, that's okay; the main job is simply telling the referee when the ball has gone out of play. He can decide who gets the throw-in.

   Remember: the entire ball has to be over the whole line. If any part of the ball is touching any part of the line, it's still in play. This is the same for the goal line.

4. Hand the referee the flag back at the end of the game and say "you're welcome" when he thanks you.

That's pretty much it. Being a club linesman isn't too demanding. But if you've got any sort of injury or chronic issue that makes light jogging or side-stepping painful, it's probably best to pass the flag to someone else.

Three Steps to Being the Right Kind of Spectator

You know the stereotypical "Bad Fan," right? He's the parent who is always screaming at the referee or the coach or even his own kid. He's the one who curses loudly. He's the one who throws up his hands and throws down his Styrofoam coffee cup if things don't go exactly as he wants.

Unfortunately, stereotypes develop for a reason and there are plenty of bad fans on soccer sidelines around the world. I've seen plenty and I bet you have, too. Sometimes you can change them and sometimes you can't. The most important thing is to make sure you never become one of them, so here's a three-step process to making sure that never happens.

Let the Coach Do the Coaching

How would you feel if you were in the middle of a big presentation at work and suddenly one of your co-workers started making comments to everyone else about how the presentation would be a lot better if you talked about something different? Even if the co-worker had some knowledge of what you were presenting, wouldn't you think he was rude?

"Sideline coaching" is basically the same thing. You could be the biggest soccer whiz since Pele and it still wouldn't be right to second-guess the coach publicly; he's the coach and he's the one making the decisions. If you don't agree with what he's doing, don't say anything about him at all and just focus on cheering for the players.

WELL DONE!

Plenty of parents think their kids should play every minute of every game, and that's understandable. They think their kid is the best. Most proud mothers and fathers do.

Dealing with playing time is a touchy issue for parents and coaches and there's no easy way to deal with it other than to try and remember something my mother always taught me: think of what the other person is dealing with.

If you're a parent who thinks your child should be playing more, it's okay to ask the coach about it—quietly, when it's just the two of you talking and not five minutes before the end of the game. Listen to the coach's explanation and, before you get all upset, try to put yourself in the coach's shoes. Is he doing his best to balance playing time for a full roster? Is he trying to balance competitiveness with having fun?

Being a coach is tough. Think about the responsibilities that come with that job before you start demanding things for your child.

If you *absolutely* have to discuss some point of strategy with the coach, the proper time is after the game when it's just the two of you—and even then, you should be inquisitive, not accusatory. If you ever become a coach, you'll appreciate other parents doing the same for you.

Let the Referee Do the Refereeing

There's probably no proof of this, but let me take a bold leap anyway: in the *history of the world,* no referee has ever made a call and then gone back and changed his mind because a parent screamed out what a blind idiot he was. It just doesn't happen.

Yet even though there's basically zero chance it will have any effect, you hear parents shouting at referees all the time. Does it make them feel better? Does it do anything at all? Truth be told, it might only serve to make the ref more irritable and less sympathetic to that particular team in the future (even if it's only unconsciously).

Most of the time, referees in youth games are people who love being around soccer and really appreciate the game. If they miss a call, it's probably because they're human beings—not because they hate your team or your child or you. They make mistakes, too, and there's probably just as good a chance that you saw the play wrong instead of them anyway.

Should you feel as though there's an epidemic of poor referees in your area, the best solution is to be proactive. Sign up for the next referee certification course and get your own whistle.

Let the Players Do the Playing

This one sort of goes without saying. Even if your daughter could hear what you're screaming at her about trapping the ball with her thigh, the odds of her understanding you, processing what you're saying, and then doing it smoothly are minimal. All she wants to hear is you yelling out, "Good job!" and "Great hustle!"

Other than that, you sort of have to take your hands off the wheel during the game. Soccer just moves too quickly and, frankly, your shouting just makes the whole game more unpleasant for everyone. Stick to the basics and everyone will be happier.

The Well-Trained Eye

Especially at younger age levels, you ought to be telling your child "good game" after the final whistle regardless of how he did on the field. It's just what parents do.

But how can you tell if little Charlie or Dan actually played well? Obviously scoring a goal is a good thing (or not allowing any for a goalkeeper), but there are some more subtle things to watch for during play that can give you a better grasp on the specifics of what your kid is doing well.

What a Defender's Good Game Looks Like

If your child plays fullback, she probably won't be scoring too many goals, so anytime her team holds the opponents to a low score it means she helped keep the defense strong.

Beyond that, look to see if she's doing a good job marking. Is she frequently clearing the ball from the penalty area to the sidelines? If so, she's stifling the opponents' attack. Is she making smooth passes to the midfielder? If so, she's helping her team go from defense to offense. Is she taking the ball away from the other team's forwards? If so, she's decreasing their possession. These are just a few of the things good defenders do.

> **WELL DONE!**
>
> Some kids may be reluctant to play fullback or midfield because the chance to score isn't as great as it is at forward. Constant encouragement from parents and legitimate praise for specific accomplishments—such as clearing crosses to the side or heading the ball to safety—are what will make these players happy with their positions instead of frustrated.

What a Midfielder's Good Game Looks Like

Midfielders' roles vary from team to team—some are more attack-minded, others lay back on defense. Either way, if your son is a midfielder he'll be responsible for moving the ball up the field and connecting his team's defenders to its forwards.

In addition to watching for your child's own shots on goal, look for good dribbling sequences, where he beats a defender and gives a teammate a scoring chance. Look for a lofted cross that results in a teammate's header. Look for a strong tackle that takes the ball back from an opponent and starts a rush.

Sometimes, the best evidence of a good game from a midfielder is how well his teammates played because he's often the one setting them up.

What a Forward's Good Game Looks Like

Goals are the obvious indicator, but soccer isn't like basketball: not everyone scores. In fact, most players don't score in a given game, even the forwards.

Sometimes a forward's best moment will be when he makes a great run to the end line and then passes the ball across the middle for a teammate to slam home. Sometimes it'll be a deft flick with his head that sends an overlapping midfielder in on goal. Sometimes it'll just be a well-placed shot that results in a tantalizing rebound for someone else.

The more an attacker makes the defense work—running, tackling, trying to keep up—the weaker that defense will become, making it easier for the offense to penetrate.

Forwards shouldn't just be judged on how many goals they score. The work leading up to the goal is just as important, even if someone else actually puts the ball in the net.

The Postgame Breakdown

Everyone reacts differently after a game. Some players like to chat, instantly analyzing what they did and didn't do; others prefer to just stew a little, playing over the game in their own minds and not wanting to verbalize much of anything.

As a parent, your role is to simply go along with whatever your child does. If he wants to talk, you can talk about what you saw in an encouraging way; if he wants to sit quietly for a bit, so be it.

The key is always to make sure the game was fun for the kid. Even those players that sulk snap out of it shortly and will start looking forward to the next game.

Parents should do that, too, because that's the best part about soccer. Even as one game ends, another one—another chance to shoot, pass, dribble, and run—is never all that far away.

The Least You Need to Know

◆ Don't be afraid to help out by being a linesman. It's fun!

◆ The best fans are the ones who are supportive and encouraging—not critics of the coach, referee, or players.

◆ Having a good game doesn't necessarily mean scoring a goal. Players contribute to a team in many ways that don't show up on the scoreboard.

Appendix A

Glossary

advantage   The decision by a referee to not whistle a foul because doing so would actually help the team that committed it.

bend   The act of curving a pass or shot in the air.

bicycle kick   A shot or pass where a player falls backward and kicks the ball over his head.

chip   A short pass that pops up in the air.

clean sheet   When a team allows no goals in a game; also called a *shutout*.

concussion   A head injury that results in a transient loss of brain function.

cross   A pass from the side of the field into the middle. Some people also call this kind of pass "centering" the ball.

cut-back   A dribbling move where a player suddenly stops his motion and turns back in a different direction.

direct kick   A free kick awarded after a foul; this kick can be shot directly into the goal.

drop ball   A restart in which the referee drops the ball between one player from each team; they must wait until the ball hits the ground before going after it.

finisher   An attacker who is particularly good at converting scoring chances.

formation   The way in which players are lined up on the field.

forward   A player who is one of the team's main attackers.

fullback   A player who is one of the team's main defenders.

give   A skill in which players move a part of their body—foot, thigh, chest—back as the ball hits it, cushioning the blow. It's an important element in trapping.

goal area   The smaller box in front of the goal. Goal kicks must be taken within it.

goal line   The line that defines the end of the field.

goalkeeper   The only player on the field who is allowed to use his hands.

half-volley   A shot or pass in which contact with the ball is made a split-second after it bounces off the ground.

indirect kick   A free kick awarded after a foul or infraction; this kick requires at least two players to touch the ball before it can be shot into the goal.

juggling   Keeping the ball in the air using your feet, legs, torso, and head—basically any part of your body that's legal for use during a game.

kickoff   The way play is restarted after a goal or at the beginning of a half. It takes place at midfield.

lead   Usually refers to a lead pass, which is a pass played out in front of the player receiving it.

mark   To cover an opponent, as a defender would to an attacker.

midfielder   A player who plays in between forwards and fullbacks. He contributes on offense and defense.

nutmeg   An old soccer term that means to play ball through an opponent's legs. You'll often hear a player who has successfully pulled it off call out "Meg!" as he runs past the hapless defender.

offside trap   A tactic in which a team has its fullbacks run up the field to try and draw the opposing forwards offside.

one-touch   A pass or shot that doesn't involve stopping the ball first.

penalty area   The larger box in front of each goal. This is the box within which the goalie is allowed to use his hands.

penalty kick   A one-on-one shot from 12 yards that's awarded when an attacking player is fouled in the penalty area.

plant   The nonkicking foot that provides stability for the player making the pass or taking the shot.

red card   The referee's signal that a player has been ejected for breaking a rule.

restart   Putting the ball back into play after the game is stopped.

run on   Catching up to a pass played out in front of you.

scissors kick   A shot or pass where a player jumps up and turns his body sideways, then kicks with his legs in a scissor motion.

shielding   When a player uses his body to block an opponent from getting at the ball.

shutout   A game in which a team allows zero goals; also called a *clean sheet*.

slide tackle   A way to steal the ball that involves sliding on the ground and hooking the ball with a foot.

split-step   A move, typically used by goalies, in which you step forward with one foot then bring the second foot up parallel in an athletic stance.

square pass   A pass that is directly to the side.

stopper   A central fullback who usually plays just in front of the outside fullbacks.

sweeper   A central fullback who usually plays just behind the outside fullbacks.

tackle   A defensive move in which one player takes the ball away from an opposing player.

touchline   The line that defines the side boundary of the field.

trap   To control the ball.

volley   A pass or shot in which contact is made while the ball is in the air.

yellow card   The referee's signal to a player that he has been warned for committing a particular infraction.

Family-Style Drills

Here's a list of a few games that parents can play at home to help their kids practice. Most require just one or two people, with some games needing a few more people (ask the neighbors!). At the end of each description, the skills that are worked during the game are listed.

Monkey in the Middle

What you need: Four players and a ball

How it works: Three players stand 10 feet apart in a triangle shape with the fourth player between them. They pass the ball around as the "monkey" tries to intercept. If he succeeds, he goes to the outside and is replaced as "monkey" by the last person to touch the ball.

Skills worked: Passing, trapping

Water Balloon Toss

What you need: Two players and a ball

How it works: A takeoff on a summertime favorite, this time you start facing each other 3 feet apart. One player tosses the ball to the other, who must trap the ball cleanly and pass it back directly to the first player's feet. Each time that sequence is successfully completed, both players take one step back. Try to see how many steps you can take back before a miss.

Skills worked: Trapping

Mini-Golf

What you need: A few trash cans, cones, or tires; two players and a ball

How it works: Set up a "course" around the backyard. One hole might be a 10-yard shot that has to knock over a trash can; another might be a lofted shot over a "water hazard" (two tires) and then a pass into a can turned on its side. Vary the challenges and the distances of each hole, and see how few "strokes" it takes to finish the course.

Skills worked: Shooting, passing

Olympic Slalom

What you need: A few cones, large rocks, or trash cans; two players and two balls

How it works: Arrange two courses alongside each other that require each player to dribble both right and left to zig-zag through it. Make it a race to see who can go through the course the fastest or, if there's only one ball, try to set a "new world record."

Skills worked: Dribbling

Index

CHECK OUT THESE
BEST-SELLERS

More than 450 titles available at booksellers and online retailers everywhere!

Grammar and Style — 978-1-59257-115-4

Word Search Puzzles — 978-1-59257-900-6

Glycemic Index Weight Loss — 978-1-59257-855-9

World Religions — 978-1-59257-222-9

History — 978-1-59257-785-9

Calculus — 978-1-59257-471-1

Positive Dog Training — 978-1-59257-483-4

Personal Finance in Your 20s & 30s — 978-1-59257-883-2

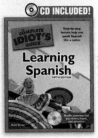

Learning Spanish — 978-1-59257-908-2

Wine Basics — 978-1-59257-786-6

Windows 7 — 978-1-59257-954-9

Music Theory — 978-1-59257-437-7

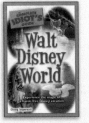

Perfect Resume — 978-1-59257-957-0

Organizing Your Life — 978-1-59257-966-2

Walt Disney World — 978-1-59257-888-7

ALPHA

idiotsguides.com